CANTON
A JOURNEY THROUGH TIME

To Sarah –
Kimberly A Kenney
Christmas 2005

Keep history alive!

Rides in "Kiddie Land" were just one of the many attractions at Meyers Lake in the 1960s. The amusement park was the crown jewel of Canton for nearly a century.

CANTON
A JOURNEY THROUGH TIME

KIMBERLY A. KENNEY

First printed 2003.
Reprinted 2004.

Published by Arcadia Publishing,
an imprint of Tempus Publishing, Inc.
Charleston SC, Chicago, Portsmouth NH, San Francisco

Printed in Great Britain.

Library of Congress Catalog Card Number: 2003111113

For all general information contact Arcadia Publishing at:
Telephone 843-853-2070
Fax 843-853-0044
E-Mail sales@arcadiapublishing.com
For customer service and orders:
Toll-Free 1-888-313-2665

Visit us on the Internet at http://www.arcadiapublishing.com

CONTENTS

ACKNOWLEDGMENTS

First, I would like to thank my colleagues at the McKinley Museum (owned and operated by the Stark County Historical Society), who have been so supportive during this whole process. The fabulous collection of photographs in the archives of the museum is truly a treasure trove of information about Canton's past. Writing a book has been a lifelong dream of mine and would not have been possible without the following individuals. I would like to thank two educators who inspired me to choose a career in history—Mr. Gary Ford, my 11th grade American History teacher at Rome Free Academy in Rome, New York, and Professor Michael Groth, my thesis advisor at Wells College in Aurora, New York. I firmly believe a student's interest in history is directly proportionate to the energy and passion of their teachers. Because of these two men, history was transformed from the realm of names, dates, and places into a wonderland of exploration about our collective human past. I will always be grateful for the foundation I received from both of them. I would also like to thank some special people in my life for their constant support, enthusiasm, and encouragement: my grandmother Marjorie Vanderhoof, my mother Cheryl Beach, my sister Kristen Beach, and my husband Christopher Kenney. Over the years, all four of them have been my biggest cheerleaders in everything that I do. Finally, I would like to dedicate this book to my grandfather, Thomas Vanderhoof, who passed away just a few days before I found out my proposal had been accepted by Arcadia Publishing. He was always so proud of me and my accomplishments, and I know he would have been even prouder still of this book.

INTRODUCTION

A highlight of the October 2002 Annual Conference of the National Council on History Education in Saratoga Springs, New York was keynote speaker David McCullough, Pulitzer Prize winning author. In his eloquent and inspiring address, he told the audience it is impossible for a historian to walk down the street and only see what there is today. Instead, historians have a keen insight into the passage of time, knowing that what we see before us is not how it always was, nor how it always will be. Time is constantly changing the landscape, writing new chapters of history.

In looking at Canton of today, little tangible evidence is left of the grand, stately homes that once lined Market Avenue. Bustling Public Square, with its wide dirt roads lined with hitching posts, has been replaced by pavement and traffic lights. No trace exists of the carefree summer days whiled away at Meyers Lake. A new Canton has replaced those cherished scenes. But they are not forgotten. Memoirs, photographs, and newspapers have captured those memories for future generations to appreciate and enjoy.

As Canton's population grew by leaps and bounds in the nineteenth century, the city began to fulfill the dreams of founder Bezaleel Wells when he laid out and registered Canton in 1805. With the opening of the Ohio & Erie Canal, trade opportunities expanded for both farmers and industrialists alike. The lucrative markets of the East Coast were now available to the people of Stark County. Though Canton was not located directly on the canal route, the boom radiated across the entire region.

Unquestionably, President McKinley is Canton's best known citizen, but the city has also been home to some of the greatest inventors and business leaders in the history of this nation. Cornelius Aultman and Joshua Gibbs helped to make this area the agricultural equipment capital of the world in the 1840s with their patented plows and reapers. Big name companies—like Dueber-Hampden, Diebold, and Timken—moved to town in the late nineteenth century, producing everything from pocket watches and safes to roller bearings. Aviation pioneers Frank Lahm and William Martin called Canton home. Professional football was born here.

CANTON

Canton is less proud of its dubious nickname "Little Chicago" in the 1920s. Underworld bosses during Prohibition controlled many communities in the Roaring Twenties, and Canton was no exception. When publisher Don Mellett used the pages of the *Daily News* to expose the criminals and their crimes, he was gunned down in his driveway on a summer night in July 1926. The subsequent investigation indicted five men, some of whom were city officials.

In both world wars, Canton won accolades for wartime production and war bond support. During World War II, Hoover was chosen as the site to build the top secret VT radio fuse, which was second only to the atomic bomb in terms of defense secrecy. Only a handful of top Hoover employees knew how to assemble all of the pieces of the VT radio fuse. The public knew nothing at all until after the war.

With the growing suburban sprawl in the postwar years, prominent downtown stores slowly abandoned their roots and opened up "satellite stores" in the new strip malls. One by one, they closed downtown stores in favor of new markets in the suburbs, proving Stark County Historian E.T. Heald's theory that the average 1950s housewife would "rather drive a mile than walk a block" to do her shopping.

The retail explosion in Jackson Township in the past decade proves that theory yet again. Almost every imaginable chain store and restaurant has a presence in Canton, reflecting the national trend away from home-owned shops to conglomerate super stores. Sears and Dillard's have replaced well-known local department stores like Stern & Mann and Vicary's. Life has become so uniform, it is often difficult to distinguish the character of individual cities and towns when traveling. They have become cookie-cutter communities, with the same architecture and businesses operating everywhere.

The key to maintaining a community's identity lies in preserving its unique past by celebrating the stories, landmarks, buildings, and historic sites that make a community different from all the rest. For Canton, this means preserving things like the McKinley National Memorial and West Lawn Cemetery, as well as properties listed on the National Register of Historic Places, including Bender's Restaurant, the Stark County Courthouse, the Palace Theater, and St. John's Catholic Church. So many important sites have already been lost to time. President McKinley's home was torn down decades ago, as were most of the grand mansions and factories built by Canton's industrial leaders. But their stories survive.

There are so many interesting aspects to the history of this city, every story could not be told in the pages of this book. Instead, *Canton: A Journey Through Time* is an introduction to the Canton of yesterday, highlighting as many personalities and events as space would allow.

Introduction

It takes imagination to appreciate history, writers painting pictures with words to show readers what life used to be like. The purpose of history is not solely to "learn from the mistakes of the past." It is more about understanding where we came from, how our ancestors lived, and how the places we know today came to be that way. History is not a single story with a beginning and an end. It is many stories, in a continuum that ebbs and flows as new resources are discovered and new perspectives are cast upon the past. History continues to unfold everyday, all around us. And the story of tomorrow is yet to be written.

Chapter One

IN THE BEGINNING

Geographically, Canton seems like an unlikely place to build a town. Situated in the middle of the wilderness, without a navigable waterway, its location was rather isolated. There was nothing but untamed forest stretching for miles, full of wild cats, wolves, and bear. In 1761, a Moravian missionary named Frederick Post was the first white man to venture to this part of the country, but the constant threat of war with Native Americans kept settlers at bay.

Two treaties helped to ease tensions and open up Ohio for settlement. Signed in 1795, the Treaty of Greenville was an agreement between the United States of America and the Native American tribes of the Wyandots, Delawares, Shawanees, Ottawas, Chippewas, Pattawatimas, Miamis, Eel Rivers, Weas, Kickapoos, Piankeshaws, and Kaskaskias. In this treaty, the tribes and settlers agreed to live in peace in the Northwest Territory. A line was drawn across the region, and the area south of that line would be open for settlement. When Ohio became a state in 1803, much of the land was still inhabited by Native American groups. In the Treaty of Fort Industry, signed on July 4, 1805, the Wyandot, Ottawa, Chippewa, Munsee, Delaware, Potawatomi, and Shawnee tribes gave up 1 million acres of land south of Lake Erie and west of the Cuyahoga River, including part of the Connecticut Western Reserve not far from the land that would become Stark County.

But Ohio was still on the edge of the frontier, with few inhabitants and only a handful of fledgling towns. Isolated settlements sprang up close to the Pennsylvania border, but the site that would become Canton was still a remote wilderness. Then a young man named Bezaleel Wells learned some inside information that made this location perfectly suited to build a town.

When he was just 15 years old, Wells moved from the bustling harbor of Baltimore to Cross Creek, Pennsylvania, a town his father founded. The newly declared republic of the United States was still fighting for independence from England at the time. Wells studied surveying and became a friend and later partner of James Ross, an influential Pittsburgh lawyer who had once worked for General George Washington. Ross had helped Pennsylvania write a state constitution. After the Treaty of Greenville was signed, Wells and Ross became some of the first customers at the new government land office established in Pittsburgh. They bought land in the new state of Ohio and founded Steubenville. Wells was then chosen to help write Ohio's state constitution and later served two terms in the state legislature as a senator.

Through his position as senator, Wells learned that a road was going to be built heading west through Ohio from New Lisbon, the county seat of Columbiana County, to the Tuscarawas River. (Part of the route is now Lincoln Highway.) He decided his new town would be located on that road, making it accessible for settlement and trade. The rich soil in the region made it an ideal spot for agricultural pursuits. Wells also knew that Columbiana County was going to be split, and the new county would need a county seat. There was a clearing with rolling plains (now known as Plain Township) at the proposed site, and it was relatively free of mosquitoes. The surrounding trees would provide ample lumber for building homes. So Wells bought 6,512 acres at $2 apiece—a bargain even in those days. President Thomas Jefferson signed his land grant.

As a young man Wells had lived in Baltimore, a busy seaport of the young United States. Hundreds of ships from around the world passed in and out of the harbor. John O'Donnell, an Irish trader in Baltimore, bought a 2,500-acre plantation and named it The Canton Estate to commemorate his first cargo to arrive from Canton, China. O'Donnell had filled his ship *Pallas* with Chinese teas, silks, satin, and other finery from the Orient. He built a showplace with deep verandahs and ample peach orchards for making brandy. Within a few months, he married the beautiful daughter of a prominent family. O'Donnell was the very definition of success. He was a hero to many of the young men in town, including Bezaleel Wells. In 1805, word came that O'Donnell had died. To honor the man he admired so much, Wells chose to name his new town Canton.

Wells laid out and recorded Canton as the first town in Stark County on November 15, 1805. He divided the town into 300 lots spread over 100 blocks, with 3 lots per block. The original settlement was located between North Street (now Sixth Street N) and South Street (now Sixth Street S). The rest of the streets between were numbered. The major street running through the center of town was to be called Market Street and would be wider than the other streets, since most of the town's business would be conducted there. The main east-west thoroughfare would be called Tuscarawas Street. The intersection between Tuscarawas and Market was the geographic center of town and would become known as Public Square. Wells named the streets running north and south after trees: Plum (now McKinley), Poplar (now Cleveland), Cherry, and Walnut. The town was located in the center of the new county, which Wells hoped would help it to become the county seat.

In the Beginning

Three blocks in the heart of Canton were not divided into lots. Wells gave these to the town as a gift, with a set of conditions to follow that are still in effect today, though the official requirements for each plot were dropped over the years. He stipulated that if the town ever reneged on the agreement, ownership of the properties would revert back to his heirs. The first block was always to be used as a school, where Timken Vocational High School is located today. The second block must always have a house of worship. The Christ United Presbyterian Church fulfills that requirement. And the third block must always be used as a cemetery. As the town grew, citizens wanted the cemetery to be located further from the center of town, so many of the early graves were moved to other plots of land. Today the original cemetery is McKinley Park, but it is said that one grave was preserved to comply with Wells's requirement that it always be used as a cemetery.

Wells employed a surveyor named James F. Leonard to lay out the lots. His chain apparently had an extra link in it, which changed the dimensions of the survey. The blocks were supposed to be 198 square feet, with each lot 66 feet wide. Instead, each block was 200 square feet with lots 66-and-two-thirds feet wide. This discrepancy caused a great deal of turmoil regarding property boundaries in later years.

Real estate prices on the eastern seaboard soared at the turn of the nineteenth century, making it difficult for many people to purchase their own land. Immigrant farmers in cities like New York, Philadelphia, and Baltimore found themselves in much the same situation they had fled in their homeland. Everyone was moving west, where land was cheap. Even some second- and third-generation settlers sold their land for a high price and came west where they could get more for their buck.

The lots in the new town of Canton were not easy to sell. There were no buildings or roads yet, which did not make the site very attractive to prospective land buyers. To encourage settlement, Wells made the terms simple. People could make a down payment on a lot and pay the rest at a later date. Some Steubenville settlers took advantage of the deal and sold their land to move to Canton. They hoped the promises Wells made would come true—that Canton would be situated on a major road and would indeed be chosen as the county seat. As a guarantee of sorts, Wells offered to refund three-quarters of the sale price if Canton did not become the county seat.

Deeds for the first six lots were officially recorded in 1808, though people began coming a few years earlier. The sale brought Wells a total of $115.75 and a population of 30 to Canton. The following year he sold 20 more lots. He purposely distributed the lots equally among the four quadrants of the town, so that no direction was favored for future expansion. When the Ohio General Assembly officially passed the act to build the state road, it was the confidence Wells needed to jump start his new town.

CANTON

The earliest settlers came to Canton from Maryland, Virginia, Pennsylvania, New York, New Jersey, and New England. Many of them were friends and acquaintances of Wells and were mostly of German descent. Some immigrants from Germany came to this area to work the fertile farmland. German and English were spoken equally in some parts of town. Some of the early settlers were hunters who squatted in makeshift cabins on land they did not own. When the plots were sold, they simply moved on.

One of the very first permanent settlers was Philip Slusser, who came to Canton in 1805 and bought land east of the original town. His daughter Elizabeth and sons Philip, Peter, and John came with him. His wife and younger children stayed in Pennsylvania for a while before following him to Canton. Slusser built Canton's first grist mill on the East Branch of the Nimishillen Creek near present-day Fourth Street SE. So Wells had the luxury of telling prospective land buyers there was a good grist mill less than a mile from the center of town. In the early days, people came from miles around to use the mill. It was so busy that customers sometimes had to wait for hours.

Meanwhile, the tiny village itself began to grow as settlers put down roots and started small businesses. Garret Crusen constructed Canton's first building on the east side of North Market Avenue in 1806. It was a small log cabin, about 18 feet square, where Crusen ran a tavern. There was a main room that was used as a bar, dining room, and kitchen. Two small additions were used as sleeping quarters. In 1807 James Leonard, Wells's surveyor, built the first brick structure in town on the southwest corner of South Market Avenue and Second Street. General George Stidger came to Canton from Baltimore the same year and started Canton's first hotel, The Courtland. Abraham Kroft opened the first store on the corner of Market and Fifth Streets. He kept his goods in the back room; customers had to walk through the front room, which was used as a kitchen, dining room, and bedroom. In 1808 Stidger built the Jacob Hentzell Travelers' Rest, later known as The Landmark Tavern, which became a favorite stopping place for people traveling along the main stagecoach route.

Soon after Stidger's tavern was built, Philip Dewalt opened The Spread Eagle Tavern on the southwest corner of South Market Avenue and West Tuscarawas Street. It was considered the finest eating establishment between Pittsburgh and Mansfield. Lodging with meals was $2.50 a week. Dewalt was famous for his beer and "pepper cakes" (described by a Martha Washington–era recipe as a wheat flour cake with coriander, caraway seeds, and ginger). In the early days, many people were coming to Canton to look for land, and as many as 20 stayed at the tavern at one time. The Spread Eagle was an important meeting place and a center for social and civic activities. Clubs, societies, and church groups met in the tavern. Traveling ministers of the Reformed and Lutheran churches held services there. It was where the founders of the town's first bank, The Farmer's Bank of Canton, met in 1815. The Thespians, Canton's first amateur theatrical group, rehearsed and gave performances there. Many traveling entertainers stopped at The Spread Eagle, including a live African lion in 1819 and an elephant four years later. The sight of such exotic animals must have been quite a show for the early settlers!

Dewalt's son Daniel attended Canton's first log cabin schoolhouse on Public Square and helped his father by caring for the horses at the tavern's stable. He also had the job of polishing the guests' boots, which they left in the hall for him after retiring for the night. Daniel was allowed to keep the money he earned from this and owned a flock of 60 sheep within five years.

The school Daniel Dewalt attended stood where the courthouse was later built. A man named Andrew Johnson from New York was hired as Canton's first teacher as soon as there were enough children in town. There were no public schools yet, so each pupil paid 25–50¢ a month to attend classes. All grades were taught in one room, as was customary at the time, with only a few books. School was in session for just three months during the winter, when children could be spared from the rigors of farm chores. Male teachers at the time earned $2 per week, while women earned only half that amount.

Canton's first post office was established in 1808 with Samuel Coulter serving as the first postmaster. Coulter had come to Canton the year before and had bought Leonard's brick building and started his tavern At the Sign of the Green Tree. The mail came once a week on horseback from New Lisbon and was kept in a drawer in the back of the bar. John Harris taught singing on the second floor of the tavern, but his enterprise did not last long because the ladies he taught refused to climb the ladder. Harris later started a debating club, became an excellent public speaker, and was eventually elected to the State Senate.

The young town welcomed its first doctor, Andrew Rappee, in 1808. Born in Paris in 1779, Dr. Rappee studied medicine at Frankfurt-on-the-Rhine and came to Baltimore in 1805. He settled in Steubenville in 1806, moving to Canton two years later. It was quite an asset to have a doctor in town, since they were few and far between on the frontier. It is possible that the presence of a doctor actually encouraged some to move to Canton. Frontier doctors had their work cut out for them, however. There were no hospitals and not very many drugs. The lack of roads meant a doctor had to travel on little more than a trail through the forest to get to his patients' homes. Like many early businessmen, Dr. Rappee often accepted goods in lieu of payment for his services.

Although Canton was laid out in 1805, Stark County was not formally founded until 1809. It was named after General John Stark, a Revolutionary War hero who had distinguished himself at the battles of Bunker Hill and Bennington. Stark was 80 years old and living on his farm in Manchester, New Hampshire at the time. He never set foot in the Ohio county bearing his name. Soon after Stark County was founded, Canton officially became the county seat. The tiny town of Osnaburg (now East Canton) was Canton's only rival, but even that was not much of a fight. The original county commissioners—John Bower, James Latimer, and John Nichols—held their first meeting on March 16, 1809 at the home of James Campbell. They appointed William Reynolds clerk, divided the county into five townships, and planned for an election for justice of the peace and all other officers. The new county needed money to build roads and bridges and to protect lives and property from wild animals and criminals. What they needed was a countywide tax.

So at their second meeting, the commissioners appointed a county treasurer and sheriff. The first county tax was set at $9 a year for taverns within the city limits and $5 a year for all other taverns. In subsequent meetings they established a 25¢ tax per year on horses and 10¢ on cattle, and a .5 percent tax on property. They also instituted bounties for wolves and panthers—50¢ for those killed under six months and $1 for older animals.

When the War of 1812 broke out, Stark County organized two companies of militia. They were stationed at Wooster for a while and were then sent to the Maumee River on guard duty and as scouts. No one from Stark County saw any action in the war. Some men were drafted into the army, but in those days one could pay a substitute to go in their place. Pioneer women were of hardy stock and often worked alongside their husbands in all kinds of work on the homestead, and Mrs. Jonathan Cable was no exception. With a young family and a farm that was not yet cleared, Mrs. Cable was nervous when her husband was drafted. Before moving to Stark County, she had worked in a tavern and had saved some money of her own. She found a substitute for her husband, but all enlistees were required to bring their own gun. Mrs. Cable was hesitant to give up the family gun because she used it to hunt turkeys and deer. She reluctantly gave the substitute her gun and $60 and kept her husband home for the duration of the war.

Though no one in Canton was killed in the War of 1812, the conflict had a significant impact on the development of the town. John Shorb's brother-in-law, Andrew Meyer, came to Canton from Baltimore after the war. He was a coppersmith and a veteran of the War of 1812, when he had equipped several ships at his own expense to assist with the war effort. In compensation for losing one of his ships while running the blockade in Baltimore harbor, Meyer received a large tract of land around Wells Lake, which was then renamed Meyers Lake. He bought 1,080 more acres from Bezaleel Wells for $11,000 and added another 3,000 acres to establish a wheat growing estate. Meyer is credited with bringing the first piano "over the Allegheny Mountains." He also built Canton's first mansion in 1817. It was constructed of local brick on the outside and imported wood on the inside.

In 1814, Wells donated 150 of the remaining lots to the Stark County Commissioners, who sold the land to raise funds for a county courthouse. Prior to the construction of the courthouse, official business was conducted in private residences or rented rooms. By 1817, the courthouse was completed at a cost of approximately $6,000. Thomas A. Drayton laid the bricks and John P. Hendley did the woodwork. The building was 44 feet square and stood on the site of the present courthouse. It occupied only one lot. It was a handsome red brick building with a roof "pitched to four sides." It had a tower with a bell that was rung three times a day—at 9:00 a.m. to summon the children to school, at noon to announce dinner time, and at 9:00 p.m. as a signal for merchants to close their stores. Just west of the courthouse the first county office building was built, housing the auditor, treasurer, recorder, and clerk.

With local government in place, the watchful eye of the press was not far behind. Fresh from mustering out of the War of 1812, John Saxton came to town when he was just 22 years old. He had lost his hearing during the war when an unsignaled cannon went off near him while he was on garrison duty. He was looking for a place to start a newspaper. He moved to Canton in 1815 with a wagon loaded with type, type cases, ink, paper, tools, and a hand press. On March 30, 1815, he published the first issue of *The Repository*, one of the earliest newspapers in Ohio, for Canton's 500 residents. It was a weekly paper and would remain that way until it became a daily in 1878. Subscriptions were $2 a year. His first editorial read, in part, "Truth shall be his guide, the publick good his aim. . . . well-informed men, of all parties, are invited to make it a Repository of their sentiments." He printed 300 papers a week.

Saxton's first big story was an account of the defeat of Napoleon at the Battle of Waterloo, published on August 24, 1815—two months and six days after it had actually happened! News traveled slowly, especially overseas. Years later, Saxton's reporting would come full circle when he wrote about the fall of Napoleon III, this time within hours of the event, thanks to the telegraph. Though the news was more timely that time around, it arrived too late for the weekly deadline. So Saxton had to save the story for the following week. It appeared in the September 9, 1870 edition.

In the early days, Saxton often bartered with the locals, giving them newspaper subscriptions in exchange for wheat, rye, beef, butter, pork, and other goods. Stark County's population was about 7,000–8,000 people at the time, and it was constantly increasing in size. In 1820, the population of Cleveland was only 606. Canton boasted seven stores, four taverns, four tan yards, a bank, nail factory, blacksmith, gunsmith, two wheelwrights and chair makers, five shoemakers, three tailors, a pottery, and several carpenters and joiners. There were also two churches, one German Lutheran and one Presbyterian. Within 4 miles of town, there were seven gristmills, three sawmills, an oil well, and two carding machines for wool and cotton. Within a decade, Canton had all of the comforts of modern civilization.

Saxton strongly opposed slavery and regularly printed abolitionist editorials. He had no competition until John Bernard founded the *Stark County Democrat* in 1833. Bernard died of cholera a few months after starting the paper, and Archibald McGregor bought it. The *Democrat* and *The Repository* editors belonged to opposite political parties, which made for lively arguments in the pages of both papers.

One of the most notable early citizens of Canton was John Shorb, who founded Stark County's first Catholic church, St. John's. He bought more plots of land from Wells than anyone else and owned many of the best pieces of property in town. Shorb was born in Zweibrucken, Germany and came to Baltimore in 1805. Like many early settlers, he moved to Steubenville in 1806 and settled in Canton the following year. Shorb opened one of the first stores in Canton in 1807. He stocked tobacco, tea, hardware, leather, drugs, gingham, and some silk. The needs of a community of 20 settlers were small, since most people made whatever they needed at home by hand. Shorb provided the bare essentials. Costs were high at that time, due to the difficulties in shipping goods from "back east." Shorb would travel to Philadelphia by horseback with his wife over the Allegheny Mountains and bring back goods in saddlebags.

Before St. John's was built, the Shorb family hosted Mass under a large oak tree that stood at the corner of Fifth Street and Shorb Avenue NW. In inclement weather, Mass was held in the front room of the Shorb home. During the construction of the church, Shorb's father was hit in the head with a beam and fell backward. He was knocked unconscious and died the next day at the age of 66. Despite the loss of one of their members, construction continued and St. John's was finished in 1824. When the "Shorb Oak" was finally taken down decades later, several relics were made and placed in the sanctuary of St. John's.

As the newly founded churches attended to the spiritual needs of the community, Canton's citizens sought to nurture their intellect by starting a library. Within a year of moving to town, James W. Lathrop helped them organize one. Lathrop was admitted to the Ohio State Bar in 1816 and opened an office in Canton. He had always been interested in books and education, so he jumped at the chance to help establish a library. Between 1815 and 1820, shares were sold at $8 apiece to raise funds to build a library. A member went to Philadelphia to purchase the first books. The titles included

Humes's *History of English America*, *Life of Washington*, *Life of Benjamin Franklin*, Locke's *On Human Understanding*, and Gibbons's *Roman Empire*. Members paid an annual fee of $3 and were allowed to take out one book every two weeks.

In 1816, Canton's residents identified another need: a bridge over the Tuscarawas River. The Kendal Tuscarawas Bridge Company constructed a wooden toll bridge at State Street. The rates were as follows: 3¢ for foot passengers; 3¢ for a horse, mule, or ass; 12.5¢ for a horse and rider; 50¢ for a wagon; 6.25¢ for each additional horse or ox; 31.25¢ for a cart, sled, or sleigh; 1¢ for hogs; sheep were free. Public mail and U.S. troops were exempt from tolls. Some townspeople objected to the bridge monopoly and started their own free bridge in 1818. That project was abandoned, and the existing bridge was made free.

Progress continued in the early years, as more people came to town and set up businesses. Another well-known settler was James Hazlett, who built a two-story brick building in the 1820s on the land that was later known as the McKinley Block. He ran a store there, selling groceries, hardware, and dry goods. Money was scarce on the frontier, so he often let people "buy" his goods in exchange for butter, milk, eggs, and other farm products. Deerskins were sometimes used as a form of currency as well. He also owned a tanning yard, which was later used by Robert Latimer as a wagon shop. Hazlett quit the business around 1843.

Another early entrepreneur, John C. Bockius, opened a shoe making shop in 1820. He made shoes to order until 1836, when he became the first merchant in Canton to sell ready made shoes. In 1830, George Michael Deuble visited Canton and found there were no watchmakers or jewelers in town. He was an immigrant from Germany, where he had learned to make clocks and watches. He moved to town in 1831, working on farms and doing whatever he could to earn some money. He started running a shop out of his home in 1833 and then opened Deuble's Jewelry in 1840. He made the first two village clocks. His sons Martin and George worked with him as apprentices and took over the family business when he retired in 1851. The Deuble family started an interesting tradition that was carried on for generations. The sons of the family were offered $500 on their 21st birthdays if they did not smoke or drink by that time. As a matter of family pride, most of the sons in the family qualified for the prize.

Isaac Harter worked for William Christmas in his dry goods store for over 10 years. He became a partner at age 21, and in 1836 when Christmas died, he took over the business and renamed it Isaac Harter & Co. He sold groceries, books, shoes, hats, and caps. He retired in 1854 and went into banking. He sold the store to David Zollars, a former employee. His bank became Canton National Bank. His sons George D. and Michael D. started the George D. Harter Bank, which would become one of the leading local banks in the twentieth century.

CANTON

Canton was incorporated as a village on January 30, 1822. James Lathrop was appointed the first president. Village officials met for the first time on May 7 of that year. They established two ordinances. The first was to "preserve cleanliness, promote safety, and prevent obstructions in the streets and alleys of the town of Canton." It required citizens to remove dead animals from the village limits and established penalties for putting stable refuse in the streets.

The second ordinance regulated the town market and the procedure for extinguishing fires. The first significant fire in town had happened the year before in February, when a house belonging to Thomas A. Drayton, the contractor who built the first courthouse, burned. At the time, John Saxton commented in *The Repository* on the lack of "engine, ladders, hooks, or buckets" in Canton. When the town fathers first tried to purchase a fire engine, they found that they could not because Canton was not incorporated. Then the rush was on to get Canton incorporated so the village could be protected against fire. Town officials authorized the purchase of a water pump fire truck called the "Phoenix" the following year. It was hand-drawn and hand-operated. The Phoenix had a reservoir, but Canton had no public water system. A bucket brigade was required to dump water into the reservoir.

The 1822 ordinance appointed a firemaster, who had the authority to command any citizen to help fight fires—with penalties for refusal. When the alarm sounded, one person from each household was expected to take a fire bucket and run to the fire. These fire buckets were often elaborately decorated and were a source of great family pride. The ordinance also stipulated a tax break for any citizen who kept two leather buckets in their home for the exclusive purpose of fighting fires.

At their second meeting in June 1822, village officials created the first local tax and appointed a tax assessor and collector. The new tax was one-half of one percent. The first penalty for violation of a village law was given that summer. John Clark was fined 25¢ for discharging a firearm within the village limits.

As the village grew, so did the need for a larger school. James Lathrop led the movement to build a new school in 1824. Canton Academy stood on the plot designated by Wells for educational purposes. It was a two-story brick structure, with two rooms on each floor that could hold about 50–60 students each. The school was known as the best in northeast Ohio. Students learned reading, writing, spelling, grammar, geography, algebra, trigonometry, and surveying.

Lathrop believed in the concept of free public education and lobbied the community to back the idea. By 1836 there were enough families who could not afford tuition, so Canton opened a public school on a trial basis. During the winter of 1837–1838, students met in the upper floor of a business owned by William Fogle on the corner of Rex Avenue and Fifth Street NE with Benjamin F. Leiter as supervisor. Leiter went on to become a lawyer, mayor of Canton, state legislator, and U.S. congressman. The first public school in Canton was declared a success.

Though Canton was located on a major road, it was not long before the citizens of northeast Ohio wanted to expand the markets for their goods beyond the local area. Counties built roads independently, so there was no statewide system of roads. None of them were paved, and some were so narrow a wagon could not even pass through them. Local farmers were producing an abundance of crops harvested from the region's rich soil. But with a finite local market, agriculture prices were extraordinarily low because of the surplus of goods. Eggs sold for 4¢ a dozen, and butter was only 6¢ a pound. The more farmers produced and the harder they worked, the greater the surplus became and the further prices dropped. Most of Stark County's farmers were living in abject poverty.

Inspired by the success of New York's Erie Canal, the state began to investigate the plausibility of constructing an inland waterway to connect Lake Erie with the Ohio River. They paid $6,000 for a feasibility study of five possible routes for the proposed canal. In the end, state officials decided to build Ohio's first canal from Cleveland to Portsmouth. The original route was to go through Akron, Canton, and Dresden. According to some accounts, the citizens of Canton decided they did not want a canal running through their town. Some say Canton's doctors objected to the canal because of fear of "ague" (malaria) stemming from the unsanitary conditions near stagnant water, which was often used as a sewer. Still others believe Captain James Duncan, who owned land west of Canton, lobbied hard for the canal route to go through his property. For whatever reason, ultimately the final route was shifted 8 miles to the west through the tiny town of Massillon.

On July 4, 1825, Ohio Governor Jeremiah Morrow invited DeWitt Clinton, New York governor and father of the Erie Canal, to the groundbreaking ceremony for the Ohio & Erie Canal at Licking Summit near Newark. A crowd of 10,000 gathered to witness the beginning of a new era for the citizens of Ohio. Clinton went on to attend the groundbreaking for the Ohio & Erie's sister canal, the Miami & Erie, in Cincinnati. Both the east and west ends of the state would soon have a cheaper, more efficient route to ship their goods.

Over 2,000 laborers were needed to complete the project, and many of the Irish immigrants who had built New York's canal were hired to work on the Ohio & Erie. To keep some of the money in the local economy, Ohioans were offered contracts to build sections of the canal as small as one-half a mile. In 1826 *The Repository* advertised for 500 day laborers to work for 30¢ a day, plus a "jigger full" of whiskey.

CANTON

The section from Cleveland to Massillon opened in 1828. Wagons came from miles around to empty their goods on canal barges or in warehouses near the canal. Between 1826 and 1836, 25 new villages were founded in Stark County because of the canal, and the local economy prospered. After the canal opened, all of the markets of the eastern seaboard were opened to Ohio's industries. It cost only $1.80 to send a barrel of flour along the canal route to New York City, where it sold for $8.

Though Canton was not located on the canal itself, the benefits of the man-made waterway radiated for miles around. By 1830, Canton had 225 homes and shops. There were three clergymen, four teachers, eight lawyers, and eight doctors. But what if Canton could build a feeder canal that connected to the Ohio & Erie? Wouldn't Canton prosper even more?

In 1828, the Sandy & Beaver Canal Company was granted a charter to build a canal between the Big Sandy Creek and the Little Beaver River. Major D.B. Douglas, a professional surveyor from the U.S. Military Academy at West Point, completed a construction plan in February 1830. The proposed canal would be 90.5 miles long with 100 locks, 7 aqueducts, and 3 feet extra depth on the summit to act as a reservoir. The most unusual aspect of his plan was a 2,700-foot tunnel through the ridge dividing the valleys of the Big Sandy and Little Beaver.

The company sold stock to finance the construction, but little was sold locally. So they went to Philadelphia to promote the cause, saying the new canal would give merchants a direct route to the markets of the "new west." They did receive some financing from Philadelphia, but the Board of Trade chose to support the Pennsylvania & Ohio Canal instead. The Board felt that the Sandy & Beaver plan did not allow for an adequate water supply to support heavy traffic during the dry season. The company hired Edward H. Gill from the Schuylkill Navigation Company to reexamine the route. He was able to add two reservoirs to the plan and shorten the route from 90.5 miles to 73.5.

When it was finally finished, the *Thomas Fleming* was the first boat to travel the new Sandy & Beaver Canal. The trip was besieged with problems. First, the boat was grounded because the water was not deep enough. Then, as they were passing through the tunnel, a large rock fell from the roof and blocked the way. Despite early setbacks, the canal did open and was used for a few years as a shipping route.

Canton tried to build a branch canal to connect the Ohio & Erie at Bolivar with the Sandy & Beaver Canal in the 1830s. It was to begin in Canton and run 12 miles southward along the Nimishillen Creek to junction with the Sandy & Beaver. It was known as the Nimishillen & Sandy Canal. A groundbreaking was held on September 18, 1835 at Walnut and North Streets. It took much longer to build than anticipated and was riddled with financial problems.

In the Beginning

The company failed—largely because of an inadequate water supply at Canton—and the canal was never finished. The ditch down Walnut Street remained open for many years as a reminder of the branch canal's failure. It was eventually filled in and the whole project was forgotten. The Sandy & Beaver met a similar fate. On April 12, 1852, the Cold Run Reservoir Dam gave way, flooding the area surrounding the canal. Locals got nervous and withdrew support. The company failed in 1853 and chunks of the canal were sold off to satisfy long overdue debts. The locks sold for more, since the stones could be reused in building projects. The railroads bought the Big Tunnel to prevent any resurrection of the canal.

As the canal brought prosperity and growth to the region, young Canton was not without its crime. Canton held its first public execution in 1833 when Christian Bachtel was hanged for killing his wife. Thousands of people came to watch him walk from the jail at Cleveland Avenue and Fourth Street SW dressed in a shroud. He was seated on top of his own coffin in a horse-drawn wagon and was escorted by soldiers to a field north of Sixth Street NE between Walnut and Cherry Streets. Two ministers preached the sermon, one in English and one in German. As the noose was tied around his neck, the sheriff said, "Christian Bachtel, your time is up, and may God have mercy on your soul." Then he sprung the trap.

Canton was also home to Dr. Lorenzo Whiting, who was instrumental in organizing the Anti-Slavery Society. He held meetings in the town hall, as "an open challenge to southern sympathizers." The first known slave was brought to Canton in 1814. John Tibbs was owned by Richard Andrews, a native of Missouri. Tibbs earned his freedom and bought a farm in Jackson Township where he lived for several years. Once the Fugitive Slave Law was passed in 1850, Tibbs sold his land and fled to Canada where he knew he would be safe from the evils of slavery. Under the new law, any federal marshal who did not arrest a suspected runaway slave could be fined $1,000. Possible runaways could be arrested without a warrant and turned over to the so-called "owner" with no more evidence than his sworn testimony of ownership. The suspected slave could not ask for a trial, nor could he or she testify on his or her own behalf. Additionally, any person helping a runway could also be sentenced to 6 months in prison with a $1,000 fine. This did not deter several local families from participating in the Underground Railroad. These families were so secretive that only a few clues exist today to prove their involvement.

In a relatively short span of time, Canton went from being a tiny hamlet in a clearing with only a handful of settlers to a bustling frontier town. Bezaleel Wells's dream had become a reality. Canton's industries were blossoming, and the population was growing. The future of the new town was alive with possibility.

Chapter Two

CANTON GOES TO WAR

In the mid-nineteenth century, Ohio represented a microcosm of society as a whole. There was a strong agricultural tradition in the rural areas and flourishing industries in the urban centers. All kinds of people were coming to Ohio—young men looking for business opportunities and land ownership, African Americans who had escaped the bonds of slavery, and immigrants pursuing their dreams in America.

This exceptional mixture of people encouraged the free flow of ideas and created a healthy political dialogue. This environment would yield several Ohio presidents in the years that followed, the first of which was William Henry Harrison. During his campaign for U.S. president in 1840, Harrison came to Massillon and stopped in Canton to eat at the Eagle Hotel. Harrison went on to win the election, but he holds the dubious record of having the longest inaugural speech—and the shortest presidency in American history. On the day of his inauguration, the weather was cold and wet. As the snowflakes blew around him, Harrison gave a lengthy speech that was over 8,000 words long. As a result, he contracted pneumonia and died less than a month later on April 4, 1841.

In the days before the telegraph, information traveled slowly across the frontier. It took three or four days for the news to reach Canton that the President was dead. The mail was still being delivered on horseback at that time, and the only other means of communication were the unreliable and unpredictable stage coach lines. The first telegraph office did not open until 1845, with George R. Saxton as its first operator.

By 1842, Canton Academy was deteriorating and was removed to make way for a new school. The English Lutheran Church paid for part of it, on the condition that they have use of the building for Sunday services and classes. The school became the Canton Male Seminary. There was also a Canton Female Seminary. Tuition per quarter at the Canton Female Seminary was $3 for the primary department, $4 for the first level English class, and $5 for the second level English class. Latin, Greek, and French were an extra $5, painting in oil and watercolors was $3, music on the pianoforte was $10, and vocal music was $1. Boarding—including all charges for room rent, fuel, and lights—was $1.50 a week. Washing was 37¢ per dozen articles of clothing.

Canton Goes to War

The separate spheres of men and women are startlingly evident in the menu of classes offered at the Canton Male Seminary during the same time period. Tuition per term for 22 weeks was $7 for Elementary English studies, and $9 each for the following: higher English courses, natural and moral philosophy, chemistry, physiology, logic, and rhetoric. An $11 fee would pay for algebra, astronomy, geology, surveying, Greek, or Latin.

The city created a Board of Education for its first Union School Plan on August 6, 1849. Canton had 500 students enrolled in public schools in 1855. There was one male teacher, whose salary was $800 a year. Each of the eight female teachers made $250 a year, again illustrating the disparity between the sexes.

Canton in the 1840s was booming economically from the success of the Ohio & Erie Canal. The canal brought new products to Canton from all over the country and across the ocean. Imported goods from Europe, finer fabrics from the East Coast, and other domestic goods like nails, glass, salt, coffee, and tea were now readily available to Canton's consumers. The advertising section of *The Repository* expanded as land sales increased and the area began to boom. From 1840 to 1850, the number of advertisers increased from 20 to 60. Although Canton was not located directly on the canal, the population still tripled from 1820 to 1844.

While the village of Canton was thriving, a national crisis was looming. In 1846, President James K. Polk sent an envoy to offer Mexico up to $20 million in return for the land that would become the states of California and New Mexico. Mexico did not want to give up half its territory, so the envoy was not received. To pressure Mexican leaders, President Polk sent General Zachary Taylor to the region. The Mexican troops viewed this as an act of aggression and attacked the Americans. Congress declared war. The President asked for 50,000 men to enlist. Ohio's quota was 2,400, and more men in Stark County volunteered than could be accepted.

Canton played a limited role in the Mexican War. Captain John Allen's "Stark County Rangers" reported for duty at Camp Washington in Cincinnati, where they were assigned to the left wing of the 3rd Regiment. They were officially known as Company K. They deployed from New Orleans to various places in Mexico, where they were assigned guard duty but saw no battle. However, several lives were lost due to fever. In total, Mexican War casualties nationwide included about 13,000 deaths, but only 1,700 died in battle. The rest were victims of disease. American forces won victory after victory and went on to occupy Mexico City. In 1848 the war was over and Mexico agreed to cede New Mexico and California in return for $15 million.

As the United States grew, by the mid-nineteenth century the railroad had become king. The Ohio & Erie Canal had been quite successful in opening up new markets, but the railroad did everything better. Early on, many believed the railroad would complement the canal system by serving to connect areas of the country where there were no canals. Indeed, early railroad lines were short, disjointed tracks used mostly for local transportation. But people soon realized tracks could be built almost anywhere, including places were it was impossible to dig a canal. It was only a matter of time before the canals would become obsolete. In a way, the canals were responsible for their own demise, since railroads were built in population centers and many of those areas owed their existence to the canals. But the railroads were faster and cheaper, and that translated to increased profits for everyone, that is, except for the canallers.

The first railroad in Stark County was the Cleveland & Wellsville Railroad, which cut across the northeast corner of the county through Alliance. The first passenger train came through on July 4, 1851. Canton had stood by and watched as Massillon blossomed when the canal came. They were not about to watch another city reap all the benefits of the railroad. *The Repository* started a campaign in favor of the railroad, publishing articles, letters, and editorials on the subject.

The Ohio & Pennsylvania Railroad (OH&PA) promised to run a line through town if Canton invested a certain amount of money in railroad stock. The town rallied and on March 2, 1852, the first locomotive of the OH&PA Lines stopped in Canton. The first passenger trains would come later, when a regular route from Canton to Cleveland was established in February 1880. The railroad made Canton's population soar in the next decades. In 1850 there were 2,600 people living in Canton. In 1860 the population had increased by 55 percent, and in 1870 by 114 percent!

As more and more of the shipping industry favored railroad cars over the old packet boats, the canals were no match for the mighty steam engines. Traffic on the canal was heavy until the late 1860s, but between 1850 and 1860, the number of miles of track in Ohio increased 10 times. By 1900, the railroad had absorbed almost all of the shipping business. The canal boom was over. New York tried to compete by widening her canals to allow for increased traffic. Ohio did not. The canals fell into disrepair and only survived through "benign neglect."

A new era was dawning for Canton in the prosperous years of the mid-nineteenth century. Farmers turned inventors would soon put Canton on the map and establish it as the agricultural capital of the world. In just a few decades, Canton and Massillon would become worldwide leaders in the production of agricultural equipment. There were three reaper and mower companies and three threshing machine companies in the area.

From the beginning of western settlement, Stark County was known for its rich, fertile farmland. In prehistoric times, a glacier had brought high quality topsoil from Canada. The glacier also left ground-up rock, which added minerals to the soil.

Canton Goes to War

Underneath the topsoil is a layer of clay. As rainfall sinks into the ground, the clay acts as a lining that keeps the water close to the plants' roots. Under the clay is a layer of sandstone and limestone, created when vast oceans covered Stark County millions of years ago. The area is also rich in coal from the ancient tropical forests that once blanketed the area in ferns, moss, and other prehistoric vegetation. These superior agricultural conditions inspired many inventors to improve upon existing designs and create new contraptions to increase output and ease the workload of the farmer.

Canton's rise to agricultural dominance began when Joshua Gibbs invented his famous patented plow in 1836. Born a Quaker in Trenton, New Jersey in 1803, Gibbs was a blacksmith, cooper, wood-working expert, and mechanic. He came to Ohio specifically to begin an agriculture business. He settled in Cleveland first but decided to move to Canton in 1824, when it was already well-known for its rich soil. At the time, Canton and Cleveland were roughly equal in population. Gibbs's improved metal plow was incredibly successful, serving customers in Ohio, Indiana, Michigan, and Illinois. When Gibbs turned the company over to his sons Lewis, Martin, and William in 1856, business was thriving. In 1870, Lewis formed a partnership with John Rex Bucher and founded the Bucher & Gibbs Plow Company. They manufactured the "Imperial Plow," as Gibbs's creation was named.

But Gibbs was not the only game in town when it came to agricultural equipment. Cornelius Aultman was born on a farm east of Canton and went to Greentown as a young man, probably as the apprentice of a wheelwright. In 1848, he built five experimental Hussey reapers. Michael Dillman, a successful farmer who lived close by, used one and was so impressed that he bought a partnership with Aultman. They went to Illinois to manufacture their reapers the following year, but Aultman soon sold his interest in the partnership and returned to Greentown.

Then Aultman started working for Ephraim Ball in his small plow shop. The two men formed a partnership in 1851 and together built 12 Hussey reapers and 6 threshing machines to sell to local farmers. Their clients were thrilled with the machines. Ball and Aultman knew they had a quality product that could be marketed nationwide. They were happy to hear the railroad was coming to Canton and quickly bought land near the tracks and moved their operations. They built a two story brick factory, with its own wood, finishing, and moulding shops.

In 1852 Ball, Aultman & Co. built 25 Hussey reapers and worked out plans for the Ohio Mower. Their success led to a great expansion in production just three years later. Tragedy struck on May 5, 1855 when a fire destroyed much of their plant. But they persevered and managed to produce 12 Hussey reapers in time for that year's harvest. Then they rebuilt their plant.

CANTON

By 1857, Ball, Aultman & Co. had produced 1,000 agricultural machines. Aultman, Ball, and Lewis Miller worked out plans for a machine to cut grass. There were two designs: one that cut the grass in front of the wheels, and one that had cutters behind. They built both, and then took their show on the road, competing in "tests" with their reapers, threshers, and mowers. The mower with cutting blades up front won first prize at a competition in Syracuse, New York, which improved their visibility and increased sales in other agricultural regions of the United States.

Ball insisted the better design housed the cutters behind the wheel, so he sold his interest in 1858 to go into business for himself, producing the alternative mower design. The original company became C. Aultman & Co. By 1860, it was the largest reaper and mower company in the world. C. Aultman & Co. was a leading industry in Canton, employing 350 men. Cornelius Aultman built his impressive residence from 1869 to 1870, between Cleveland Avenue and Market Street and Ninth and Eleventh Streets.

As Canton became a leader in the agricultural industry, several mercantile establishments were also active in town. By 1854, Canton had been incorporated as a city with a population of 40,000. On the eve of the Civil War, merchants lined Tuscarawas Street. John S. Shilling & Augustus Herbruck sold dry goods, groceries, Queensware, books, and shoes. Schweitzer & Wikidal carried hardware, cutlery, and paint. William P. Prince & J.R. Raber sold furniture, cabinetware, and glasses—and were undertakers as well. At Meyer & Sol Fisher a silk hat was only $1.50. John Danner was selling sewing machines for $38 each.

John F. Raynolds founded the Canton Gas Company in 1855. People were slow to convert to gas from kerosene because gas light tends to flicker as it burns, making it difficult to read or sew by. Even those homeowners who did convert to gas kept some kerosene lamps for these activities. The city installed gas street lamps around Public Square. Later, when Raynolds died in 1889, a group of capitalists from out of town purchased his company and renamed it the Canton Gas Light & Coke Company.

Flickering gas lights conjure up images of nostalgic family gatherings around the holidays, especially Christmas. With origins in Germany, the holiday had been celebrated in parts of Europe for decades. Given the concentration of German settlers in Canton, it is odd that no Christmas celebrations were held in the early days of the city. It is likely that most families of German descent observed the holiday themselves quietly, without much public fanfare. Nevertheless, early issues of *The Repository* show no special Christmas services, and all the stores, courts, and public offices remained open. Business proceeded as usual on December 25. The first allusion to Christmas did not come until 1843, when it was mentioned in reference to a concert by the Odeon Association.

No stores advertised Christmas presents until 1852. Danner was selling albums and books for the "holidays." Saxton featured a great variety of "Holliday presents." And J.J. Fast & Son advertised Christmas and New Year presents "in all variety" at their "cheap book store." Very few stores mentioned the holiday for the rest of the 1850s. In 1857, *The Repository* wished readers a "Happy Christmas" for the first time. In 1860, the newspaper grouped Christmastime ads together under a banner that read "Holliday Presents." An 1861 editorial mentioned Santa, and stores closed for Christmas for the first time the following year. By 1868, *The Repository* featured a large supplement specifically for Christmas, and most of the merchants in town took out an ad. Churches began to have services. In just a decade, Christmas was transformed from an unobserved day to a major holiday.

As Canton cultivated warm Christmas traditions, a clash of ideologies was tearing the nation apart. In the heady days before the Civil War, there was much debate about the morality of slavery, the legality of secession, and the gloomy prospect of a country at war with itself. *The Repository* firmly supported the North and abolition. Editorials of the time period hoped for a peaceful settlement to the conflict.

In Canton, two companies of state militia had organized a few years earlier. They were known as the Canton Zouaves and the Canton Light Guards. The 107th Regiment of the Union Army, headed by Colonel Seraphim Meyer, was made up mostly of Cantonians of German descent. Canton soldiers fought in every major battle of the war.

At home, people participated in the usual war efforts. Women's Aid Societies made bandages and hospital supplies. Three out of every five men aged 20–40 were in the service. Women left alone often went out to find work to support their families in the absence of their husbands.

When the war was over in 1865, slavery was vanquished, over 600,000 Americans were dead, and the South lay in ruins. It was time for the nation to regroup, rebuild, and refocus on the future. But people also wanted to preserve the memory of the nation's greatest conflict. Since Lincoln had called the Union Army his "Grand Army," it was fitting to call the Civil War veteran's organization the "Grand Army of the Republic" (GAR). Dr. B.F. Stephenson organized the first post of the GAR in Decatur, Illinois on April 6, 1866. Soon after, posts sprang up in Wisconsin, Indiana, Iowa, Missouri, and Ohio. Canton Post No. 25 was founded December 15, 1879 with the following charter members: H.R. Dittenhoffer, T.H. Phillips, W.A. Wikidal, P.S. Sowers, John Webb, Michael Alder, W.O. Meyers, T.W. Saxton, L.S. Ensign, H.C. Ellison, Jacob Kuneman, J.M. Ebersole, R.G. Garber, A.T. McCutcheon, W.F. Reynolds, Joseph Craig, J.H. Weidman, and W.S.S. Erb. The preamble of the Rules & Regulations of the GAR outlined their purpose:

CANTON

We, the soldiers and sailors, and honorably discharged soldiers and sailors, of the Army, Navy, and Marine Corps of the United States, who have consented to this Union, having aided in maintaining the honor, integrity, and supremacy of the National Government during the late rebellion, do unite to establish a permanent association for the objects hereafter set forth. . . .

The GAR lists Fraternity, Charity, and Loyalty as the objects of their organization. They sought to "perpetuate the memory and history of the dead," "to assist such comrades in arms as need help and protection," and "maintain true allegiance to the United States of America." The local GAR hosted several events over the years.

The Grand Army Band was organized in 1866, 13 years before the local GAR post was established. Though it was not directly affiliated with the GAR, a core group of Civil War veterans were charter members. When Charles Fiala came to town in 1869, the band had no leader. Fiala was the son of a Bohemian musician and had been trained in Europe for a career in music. He took over the Grand Army Band, and the group quickly gained a reputation for being one of the finest music groups around. An octagonal bandstand was built at Public Square in 1874, and the band gave concerts there regularly. Band members wore white trousers, long black boots, and white helmets trimmed in brass.

In 1876, Fiala took the band to the Philadelphia Centennial where they competed with bands from all over the country. In 1901, the Grand Army Band was invited to play for the Confederate Veterans' Reunion in Dallas, Texas. It was the first time a northern band had been asked to participate in a Confederate gathering. But the band earned its greatest fame playing for William McKinley's many campaigns. They played for all of his congressional campaigns except the one he lost. They also played for the conventions where he was nominated for governor and for president.

Thayer's Military Band, a rival of the Grand Army of the Republic, was started by H. Clark Thayer and William E. Strassner. Thayer was a professor at the Dana School of Music in Warren, Ohio. He saw opportunity in the growing city of Canton, so he moved to town and began teaching private lessons. He joined the Emerson Orchestra, a popular group that was regularly booked for dances. Strassner was born in Orrville in 1874 and joined the Orrville Band when he was just 13. His brother Edgar also played with the group. In 1890 the family moved to Canton so the boys' father, Reverend Frederick Strassner, could take over as pastor of the First Reformed Church of Canton.

Native Cantonians George and Ernest Jones started taking lessons from Thayer and played in a brass quartet with the Strassner boys. They decided to start their own band, holding their first meeting at Thayer's studio on the southeast corner of Cleveland Avenue and Sixth Street NW. About 12 musicians came to that initial meeting. As the group grew, it became known as "the brotherhood" because so many sets of brothers played in it.

Thayer's Military Band gave its first public performance in 1892 for Decoration Day (now Memorial Day) celebrations. Over the years, Thayer's Military Band and the Grand Army Band competed for engagements and often played at the same major events. When Thayer's disbanded in 1941, six of the earliest members totaled 244 years of band membership collectively.

Following the Civil War, a group of young men formed the Canton Cadets, a volunteer drilling team that practiced military exercises in the midst of peacetime. Impressed by the spectacle of the Decoration Day parade of 1876, a dozen boys aged 10–13 decided to form a cadet company. They marched with wooden guns, following strict military drilling protocols up and down the streets of Canton. They made their first public appearance the following year in a Memorial Day parade. Historian John Danner noted in his scrapbook, "No single feature of the procession which marched to the cemetery yesterday was more attractive than the little cadets, whose trim, neat appearance and soldierly bearing were the admiration of all beholders." Members of the group forged lifelong friendships, inspired through patriotism, honor, and duty. The Canton Cadets continued to meet regularly for several years, becoming a source of community pride for the city of Canton. Today on a walk through West Lawn Cemetery, you can still see metal grave markers highlighting members of the Canton Cadets.

As the Canton Cadets kept themselves out of trouble with their military drilling, many other kinds of entertainment were gaining popularity in the postwar period. Louis Schaefer, perhaps one of Canton's most colorful and influential citizens, recognized a need in the community and set out to fill it. Schaefer was born in Alsace-Lorraine and trained as a lawyer, emigrating to the United States in 1830. In February 1867, Schaefer announced plans to build an Opera House in Canton. At the time, Comstock's in Columbus was the only opera house in the state. The town was divided about this proposed addition to their community. The English-speaking churches were very much against it. The German-speaking churches, Catholics, and non-churchgoers were in favor of it. Plans moved forward, and 150 couples attended the Opera House's grand inaugural ball in February 1868. The Opera House hosted some "high class events," including *Hamlet*, *The Merchant of Venice*, and *Uncle Tom's Cabin*. Other popular shows included *The Streets of New York*, *Ten Nights in a Bar Room*, *Rip Van Winkle*, and *Davy Crockett Making His Last Stand at the Alamo*. Tickets sold for 25¢ to 50¢ a piece.

CANTON

Schaefer tended to like people in the entertainment business and they liked him. Many well-known actors of the period brought their plays to Canton, though they often overlooked other towns of similar size. As a result, Cantonians were able to see first-rate theatrical productions, right in their own town.

Some of the churches began to come around when they realized the Opera House could be used for benefits, festivals, and even preaching services. *The Repository* ran an editorial saying there was no harm in dancing or going to the theater, but many pastors and churchgoers remained skeptical. In response to these complaints, Louis Schaefer, a boisterous and popular figure, brought Robert G. Ingersoll to Canton to give an atheistic lecture. He purposely scheduled the lecture for a Sunday night and even hired a band to play on the balcony to attract more people, some of whom were headed to evening church services.

Schaefer also set up his own lecture on Noah's Ark, where he ridiculed the Bible story of the flood. The show consisted of an empty stage with a little red and yellow ark with wooden figures of Noah and pairs of animals. The lecture was reportedly hysterical and wildly popular, though it won him no favor with Canton's churches.

Even though he was quite a character, Schaefer was also very active in the civic affairs of Canton. One of his most significant achievements was the establishment of a city water system. In January 1868, a hellish fire destroyed five significant stores downtown. Clearly Canton needed more equipment for fighting fires. Schaefer agreed to chair the committee to buy a new steam-powered fire engine. But just like the first fire engine, there was an inadequate water supply to power the new one.

It was decided that Meyers Lake would be an excellent source of water, and plans were made to build a stone intake structure from the east side of the lake that would flow to the pumping station in Waterworks Park. As we shall see later, Schaefer was also responsible for convincing John C. Dueber to move his successful company to Canton.

Schaefer also led the movement for a new courthouse. Agitation for remodeling and expanding the courthouse began as early as 1833, not long after its completion. The cornerstone was laid July 4, 1868 before a crowd of 3,000. It was made entirely of Stark County materials, including the masonry, iron doors, slate roof, brick, and cut stone. At 113 by 110 feet, it was much larger than the original building, which was only 44 feet square. The $113,600 building was dedicated on Washington's birthday in 1870. Bells rang out, high school students sang, and cannon boomed as trainloads of people came from as far away as Jersey City, New Jersey and Pittsburgh. One thousand people dined at St. Cloud's Hotel.

In 1893, just 23 years after the "new" courthouse was built, it was again too small for the growing community. So the commissioners made plans to remodel it. The renovations were so extensive, one could argue the structure was actually rebuilt. A west wing was added, the old walls were encased in stone, and fireproof vaults were added for records. It was during this renovation when the two separate towers were replaced by one tower, surrounded by four "Trumpeters of Justice," better known as the courthouse angels. It cost between $175,000 and $200,000.

Despite the "temptations" of the Opera House, the morality of Canton's citizens was alive and well. The Canton YMCA is the oldest in Stark County, and one of the six oldest in the state of Ohio. It held its first meeting on April 16, 1866 in the lecture room of the Methodist church. The week before, the ministers of Canton's eight Protestant churches announced plans for the gathering. The first YMCA rooms and library opened on March 13, 1867 on East Tuscarawas. The library was comprised of 800 volumes and was open every evening except Sunday from 6:30 to 10:00. It was free to all.

The YMCA hosted six lectures in 1867, featuring some of the best speakers in the country. Season tickets for the 1867–1868 lecture series were $1.50 per person, $2.50 for a gentleman and a lady, and $3.50 for a family. In 1868, the YMCA competed with the Opera House for the attention of Canton's youth, as the Opera House became the center of cultural, social, and intellectual life. As we shall see, a young, energetic William McKinley would breathe new life into the YMCA—and bring international attention to Canton.

Chapter Three

THE MCKINLEY YEARS

Although Canton claims William McKinley as the city's favorite son, he was born somewhere else. He was born in the sleepy hamlet of Niles, 55 miles northeast of Canton, on January 29, 1843. He moved to Poland, Ohio when he was just nine years old, and spent his youth there until enlisting in the Civil War. McKinley came to Canton as a young adult and called this city home through several terms as congressman (1877–1884 and 1885–1891), two terms as governor, and finally two terms as President of the United States.

McKinley was the seventh of nine children born to William McKinley Sr. and Nancy Allison McKinley. His family lived in a modest two-story frame house on the upper floor of a country store. (That home was destroyed by fire in 1937, and the Poland home was torn down in the 1890s.) All of the McKinley children were encouraged to read every night after dinner.

At the age of 17, McKinley went to Allegheny College in Meadville, Pennsylvania, but he became sick and returned home. He took a job teaching in a one-room schoolhouse, earning $25 a month. After staying for one term, he became the assistant postmaster of Poland in early 1861.

Since both of his grandfathers had served in the War of 1812, McKinley continued the family tradition of military service. He enjoyed a distinguished career in the Civil War, earning the title of brevet major. He enlisted as a private in Company E of the 23rd Regiment of the Ohio Volunteer Infantry (OVI) in June 1861. He was sworn into service by General John C. Fremont, known as "The Pathfinder." After his first taste of warfare pursuing Confederate guerillas in western Virginia, he wrote in his diary: "It may be that I will never see the light of another day. Should this be my fate, I fall in a good cause and hope to fall in the arms of my Blessed Redeemer."

McKinley not only survived four years of service in the Civil War, he was never even wounded, though he saw serious combat at the battles of South Mountain and Antietam. He was promoted to commissary sergeant on April 15, 1862. Several promotions followed, including second lieutenant in September 1862 and first lieutenant in February 1863. He earned the rank of captain in July 1864 and finally major in March 1865. He mustered out on July 26, 1865.

Following the war, he enrolled at Albany Law School, graduating in 1867. He was admitted to the Ohio State Bar and was looking for a place to settle down and open up his own practice. At the urging of his sister Anna, who had come here to teach school, McKinley came to town in 1867. Canton was booming in the years following the war, with many opportunities for a bright, young lawyer. McKinley had several prominent lawyer and judge friends who sent recommendations and introductions for him. Coincidentally, Judge George W. Belden was looking for a partner at the time. The two formed a partnership—Belden & McKinley. The Major, as he was sometimes called, became involved in local politics and community organizations immediately.

McKinley gave his first political speech at a Republican meeting in North Canton, dazzling the crowd with his eloquence. It was the beginning of a long and successful career that would be tragically cut short at its apex. But in the 1860s his life was full of promise, and he impressed everyone who came in contact with him. Once at the Canton Literary Club, sponsored by the YMCA, McKinley participated in a debate on woman suffrage. He argued for it convincingly, and when his 10 minutes were up the crowed wanted to hear more. He continued for another hour!

McKinley was elected president of the YMCA on May 20, 1868. He launched a series of Saturday evening street meetings at Public Square, where people sang hymns, listened to pastoral addresses, and prayed. Through his leadership, the Y secured the donation of a 10-year lease on the third floor of the First National Bank Building. The bank even paid to have the rooms painted and provided steam heaters and gas fixtures.

McKinley also became a member of the local Masonic Temple. He had joined in Winchester, Virginia during the war. At the age of 25, McKinley was elected county prosecutor. By then he was regularly speaking on behalf of the Republican Party throughout Stark County.

McKinley was not in town long before he caught the eye of Ida Saxton, granddaughter of *The Repository* founder John Saxton. Ida was the belle of Canton and was intrigued by the dashing war hero. She was working as a teller in her father's bank at the time, after returning from a grand tour of Europe with her sister. She and McKinley were married on January 25, 1871. It was the first event held in the new Presbyterian Church, which was not even completed yet. There were 750 guests, including Governor Rutherford B. Hayes, who would later become President as well. The couple were honored with a dinner party at the home of the bride's parents before departing on a three week honeymoon trip to New York. Sadly, Ida's grandfather was too sick to attend the festivities. He died in April of that year. By common consent, Canton's businesses were closed for his funeral. He was buried next to his wife in West Lawn Cemetery.

Six months after the wedding, McKinley lost his re-election bid for county prosecutor by 45 votes. For four years, he practiced law on his own and was not involved in the political scene. Though those years were fulfilling professionally, in his personal life he and Ida faced several challenges. After the deaths of Ida's grandfather in 1871 and her mother in 1873, the McKinleys were dealt a blow from which Ida would never recover. Their youngest daughter, Ida, died in infancy in 1873. The older daughter, Katie, had heart trouble and died in 1876. Ida began to suffer from periods of severe depression, complicated by digestive problems, phlebitis, and fainting spells that were later diagnosed as epilepsy. She busied herself crocheting an estimated 4,000 pairs of slippers, which she gave to friends or donated to charities.

Despite personal setbacks, Ida encouraged her husband to continue in politics. He worked on Rutherford B. Hayes's campaign for governor of Ohio, making many prominent friends along the way. In 1876 he ran for Congress, when he was just 33 years old. He was well known in the community and well liked by all who knew him. Miners were among his most staunch supporters for his victory on their behalf during a lawsuit concerning their strike. He campaigned throughout the congressional district, including Stark, Carroll, Columbiana, and Mahoning Counties. A doctor with a large practice drove him around and introduced him to his patients. A businessman took him to barbershops and storekeepers to meet as many voters as possible. He won the nomination in every township in Stark County but one.

McKinley's platform was a protective tariff and sound money—two issues he would champion throughout his political career. He won the election and spent 14 years in Washington, serving in the 45th through 51st Congress. He reportedly visited Ida frequently, whenever he could steal a few minutes to be with her.

Early on, McKinley began his fight for a protective tariff. In 1877 the Wood Tariff Bill was introduced, calling for a reduction in tariffs. McKinley was strongly opposed to it. He made his first speech in the House on April 5, 1878. Stark County Historian E.T. Heald writes, "He attacked the bill squarely, and, without oratorical flourish, presented his arguments in clear, concise and convincing terms." The Wood Bill was defeated. He continued his battle by writing his own legislation—The McKinley Tariff Bill. The bill called for record high tariffs on imported goods, which was designed to protect American industries from foreign competition. The McKinley Bill, as it became known, passed in 1890.

McKinley enjoyed tremendous success throughout his years in Congress, making friends who would benefit his career in the years to come. He became a leading speaker for the Republican Party, earning himself opportunities at every turn. President Garfield recommended him for the Ways and Means Committee and he was appointed in 1880.

The McKinley Years

After losing his bid for re-election to Congress by 300 votes in 1890, largely as a result of gerrymandering by the Democratic Party, people began to speculate about the governor's race. McKinley was apprehensive about running because the Democrats were so entrenched, and he feared a loss might compromise his future in politics. In the end, he decided to take a chance. McKinley's campaign for governor of Ohio began August 1, 1891. He traveled for three months, giving two to twelve speeches a day in 86 of 88 counties. He won the election 386,739–365,288 and was inaugurated on January 11, 1892. He served two two-year terms.

Soon the party was talking about nominating him for the Presidency. McKinley agreed to run but did not attend the nominating convention. Instead, he stayed in Canton and listened to the convention via telephone from his home. The executive committee of the Business Men's Association arranged for a fire alarm box to be placed in *The Repository* editorial room. When McKinley received the number of votes he needed to win the nomination, the bell would ring 98 times—the total number of voting delegates. As the roll call was read, McKinley must have been straining to listen, heart pounding, yet reserved in his typical manner. When they got to Ohio, he already had 421 votes, and he only needed 453 to win. Ohio's 46 votes officially gave him the nomination, which must have made it even more special to him. In the end, he received 661 votes.

When the announcement of his nomination was made, people were supposed to go to Public Square for a celebration. Instead, an impromptu gathering at the residence began to form. The crowd was whipped into a frenzy, and some even tried to get into the house. McKinley came out to address them, giving what is known as his first Front Porch Campaign speech. The morning after, *The Repository* reported on the scene the night before, saying "not a picket remained in the fence around the McKinley yard . . . all had been carried away by the 50,000 celebrants and souvenir hunters." Indeed it was the beginning of a wild ride for the people of Canton.

Early on, McKinley decided that he would not campaign around the country like his opponent William Jennings Bryan was doing. Instead, he would remain at his home in Canton and would receive trainloads of visitors from around the country. His campaign manager Marc Hanna organized the delegations, so McKinley knew exactly when each group was coming. This enabled him to tailor his speeches to the needs and concerns of that specific group of people. McKinley shook hands with everyone who made the trip to see him. Murat Halstead, a famous newspaper reporter of the period, described the experience of shaking the candidate's handshake:

> It allures the caller, holds him an instant, and then quietly and deliberately
> "shakes him." The hand goes out straight for you, there is a warm pressure

of the palm, a quick drop, a jerk forward, and the thing is over. There is something besides the extended palm to allure you, and that is Mr. McKinley's beaming countenance. When greeting the public he never ceases to smile. It is not a forced smile, it invites you forward and compels your own smile in spite of yourself.

He greeted thousands in this manner, right from his front porch. He prepared each speech carefully and required the delegation speakers to be just as diligent in their speeches. Every speaker was required to submit the text of their speech to McKinley himself in advance of their trip to Canton.

McKinley ran on the same platform he had always used—a protective tariff and sound money. In the beginning, he believed that the tariff issue was the most important in the election, saying, "I am a tariff man standing on a tariff platform. The money matter is unduly prominent. In 30 days you won't hear anything about it." Judge William R. Day disagreed, saying "In my opinion in 30 days you won't hear anything else." Day was right. Both candidates concentrated heavily on the money question. Bryan advocated the free coinage of silver, preaching that the American people "shall not be crucified upon a cross of gold." McKinley championed the gold standard, and his supporters wore gold bug pins and formed "Sound Money Clubs."

Canton greeted thousands of visitors every day during the campaign, and the citizens were happy to do so. All of the excitement put Canton on the map, and the visitors spent money in Canton, boosting the local economy. The saloons did very well. An arch was constructed at the intersection of Market Avenue and Sixth Street, outfitted with electric lights and a portrait of McKinley, to welcome all of the visitors.

Delegations representing all kinds of groups flowed in and out of Canton. In addition to delegations from individual states, people also came in special interest groups, including businessmen, working men, miners, men of foreign birth, first time voters, southerners, religious societies, political clubs, marching clubs, bankers, tradespeople, manufacturers, railroad men, streetcar employees, soldiers, lawyers, doctors, and college students. Although women would not get the vote until 1920 with the passage of the 19th Amendment, women's groups still came as delegations. It was believed that the women held some influence over the votes of their husbands, so they were courted like any other political group. To accommodate the influx of people, the Traffic Association gave record low rates on train fare for groups of 40 or more coming to Canton. The Saturday before the election was the busiest day of the entire campaign—20,000 voters in 26 delegations came.

The McKinley Years

On Election Day, McKinley voted at Precinct B of the 1st Ward at 8:55 a.m. with his brother Abner and Sam Saxton. It was a tense day in Canton as the entire nation awaited the results of the election. Would the Front Porch Campaign win out over the 18,000 miles Bryan had traveled in three months, speaking to an estimated 5 million people? Would Canton become the home of the 25th president of the United States? Company I of the Ohio National Guard was posted on top of the courthouse and was instructed to fire the presidential salute of 21 rounds as soon as the election was declared in McKinley's favor. Finally, at 1:00 a.m. McKinley gave the signal. He had won the election. McKinley received 7,111,697 votes and 271 electoral votes to Bryan's 6,509,052 and 176.

One of William McKinley's biggest supporters throughout his campaign was William Rufus Day, a prominent Canton attorney who would serve as secretary of state and later become an associate justice of the Supreme Court. Born in Ravenna in 1849, Day was admitted to the bar in 1872 and began his career in Canton, a growing town with a population of 10,000. He formed a partnership with William A. Lynch, who began as a partner of Louis Schaefer, concentrating on trial cases and corporation law. Day soon married Schaefer's daughter Mary.

In 1889, President Harrison offered Day a U.S. judgeship. Though he was confirmed by the Senate, Day declined for health reasons. When he was elected President, McKinley offered him the position of attorney general, but he declined that as well for "personal reasons." Before long, Day would receive an opportunity he could not pass up.

Right after his inauguration, McKinley had an emergency in the State Department. Secretary of State John Sherman, who was 74 years old, was not doing well. His health and memory were failing him. McKinley appointed Day as assistant secretary of state, which carried the burden of all the responsibilities of secretary of state without the title. Day took the offer and went from a salary of $15,000 as a private lawyer to $4,500 as a high ranking government official.

McKinley's first major presidential problem was handling the mounting crisis in Cuba. A bloody civil war between Cuba and Spain was threatening American sugar plantations. War mongers in the United States called for action against Spain, but McKinley proceeded with caution. As a Civil War veteran, he had seen unimaginable suffering firsthand on the front, and he was not about to engage the country in another conflict without just cause.

One of the most vociferous war agitators was Theodore Roosevelt, who would later become McKinley's running mate after the death of Vice President Garret Hobart in 1899. Roosevelt was anxious to go to war, mostly because of his personal desire to become a war hero. He spoke out publicly whenever he could, even making derogatory comments about the President. He once said McKinley did not have "the backbone of a chocolate éclair."

Then on February 15, 1898, the USS *Maine* blew up in Havana Harbor. People rallied around the slogan "Remember the Maine!" Newspaper publishers William Randolph Hearst and Joseph Pulitzer immediately accused Spain of attacking the United States Navy, writing a series of stories of dubious origin dubbed "yellow journalism." When a court of inquiry found that the explosion was caused by a sunken mine, McKinley finally accepted that the only way to ensure the permanent independence of Cuba was to go to war with Spain. Modern day forensic research has disproven that theory, instead citing that the explosion was indeed an accident. But at the time, backed by the official court of inquiry, everyone—including the President—was convinced that Spain was to blame. When McKinley declared war against Spain in 1898, Sherman resigned. Day stepped up to full status as secretary of state, "for the duration of the war."

The war took just 113 days and completely destroyed the Spanish fleets in Cuba and the Philippines. The United States emerged as a world power, with imperialist problems. The war cost a total of $300 million and added 124,000 square miles to American territory. As a result of the war, McKinley signed the annexation of Hawaii on July 7, 1898, and Guam became a possession of the United States.

When the war ended, the United States was in uncharted waters as an emerging world power. Day was involved in shaping the new policies that would govern the shift from isolationism to imperialism. As soon as a peace protocol was signed on August 12, 1898, Day resigned as secretary of state. McKinley immediately appointed him president of the U.S. Peace Commission. Day went to Paris to meet with the Spanish commissioners to work out details of the peace treaty. It was signed by both sides in December. Day planned to return home to Canton, but again McKinley tapped his talents and appointed him to a federal judgeship in the 6th Judicial Circuit, which had jurisdiction over Michigan, Ohio, Kentucky, and Tennessee. The presiding judge was William Howard Taft, who had been appointed at the young age of 32.

McKinley finally saw the victory of sound money when the Gold Standard Act was passed on March 14, 1900. It was made possible in part by the discovery of gold in the Klondike, which nearly doubled gold production in this country.

McKinley was unanimously renominated at the Republican Convention in Philadelphia in June 1900. The biggest issue facing the party was convincing Teddy Roosevelt, then governor of New York State, to accept the nomination for vice president. Garret Hobart, McKinley's running mate in the 1896 election, had died during the first term. The convention dragged on and on as the delegates tried to persuade Roosevelt. The Grand Army Band was playing for the convention, and the band's manager started to get worried about the musicians missing extra days of work. Many of the boys were employed at Dueber-Hampden, so the band manager wired John C. Dueber to inform him of the delay. Dueber replied, "By all means, stay until the convention is over. Then go to Washington DC and serenade the President!" When the convention finally concluded, the band went to Washington and found the Marine Band giving a concert at the White House. The Marine Band stepped aside and let Canton's Grand Army Band give a concert of their own. When McKinley was free, he came out to greet the group and gave each band member a cigar.

After his re-nomination, McKinley again refused to campaign, saying that it was not "presidential" to do so. He beat William Jennings Bryan a second time, gaining a larger margin of victory. This time McKinley won 7,219,525 popular votes and 292 electoral votes to Bryan's 6,358,737 and 155.

Following the second inauguration in January 1901, McKinley planned to tour the Pacific Coast. But Ida became ill and their plans were cancelled. Instead, they stopped in San Francisco where she lingered between life and death for two weeks. She eventually recovered and returned to Washington, and then went on to Canton for the summer. The President joined her. They enjoyed spending time in their home on North Market Avenue and were looking forward to retiring there when McKinley finished his second term.

The President and Mrs. McKinley left for the Pan American Exposition in Buffalo, New York on September 4, 1901. On Friday, September 6 they spent the morning with friends and went to see Niagara Falls. The day before was "President's Day" at the Exposition, and McKinley had delivered what many said to be his greatest speech. It was in that speech that he made the famous quote that is now immortalized on the interior of the McKinley National Memorial: "Let us ever remember that our interests are in concord, not conflict; and that our real eminence lies in the victories of peace, not those of war."

At 3:30 in the afternoon he arrived on the grounds of the Expo. Mrs. McKinley took a carriage to the Milburn Home. The President continued on to the Temple of Music with John G. Milburn and his secretary George Courtelyou, where he was scheduled to meet with "the people." The organ bellowed out the national anthem as they arrived. The President took his place at the end of the room, with Milburn on his left and Courtelyou on his right. Law enforcement officials were everywhere, including the Secret Service, local detectives, and a detail of a corporal and ten army soldiers. They were instructed to keep their eyes on everyone who stood in line to meet the President.

CANTON

The line followed one after another, with the President shaking the hand of everyone who passed by. According to eyewitnesses, a man came up to the President and held his hand longer than was necessary for a cordial handshake, which drew the attention of some of the guards. They intervened and asked him to move along. The man behind him had a bandaged hand, but received little notice because of the commotion in front of him. Seeing the bandaged hand, the President reached for the man's other hand. Suddenly a gun went off. The President had been shot twice at point blank range—the bandage had concealed a .32 caliber hand gun. It was 4:07 p.m.

At first, McKinley did not realize what had happened. He fell backwards. Immediately the security detail jumped on the man with the bandaged hand, beating and kicking him. Despite having just been shot by this man, McKinley urged them to stop, saying "Don't let them hurt him." Then he said to his secretary, "My wife—be careful, Courtelyou, how you tell her—oh, be careful."

The assassin's name was Leon Czolgosz, an anarchist who saw McKinley as the enemy of the working class. Later on in his trial, it came out that he had been stalking the President for quite some time, even following him on afternoon excursions to Meyers Lake in Canton. He was a deranged man who had originally wanted to kill the President in Cleveland. But his parents lived in Cleveland and he decided he did not want to disgrace them by shooting the President in their town. In his signed confession, Czolgosz stated that he had been inspired by a speech by anarchist Emma Goldman.

An ambulance rushed to the scene and transported McKinley to an emergency hospital on the fairgrounds just 11 minutes after the shots were fired. He had sustained two wounds. The first bullet hit him between his second and third ribs, a little to the right of the sternum. The second bullet struck him deep in the abdomen, piercing the stomach walls twice. That wound was far more serious. Dr. Matthew D. Mann administered ether to the President around 5:20 p.m. As he trailed off, he was reciting the Lord's Prayer.

The surgeon could not locate the second bullet and was forced to sew him up without removing it. The President was taken to the Milburn home still unconscious. Despite her chronic health problems and general fragility, Ida surprised everyone with her courage and strength during this crisis.

The first telegraph about the shooting reached Canton at 4:35 p.m., 21 minutes after it had happened. The news reached the county fairgrounds just before the fourth heat of a horse race was scheduled to run. McKinley had been the guest of honor at the County Fair just a few days before he left for Buffalo. Everyone was in shock. Resolutions of sympathy were immediately drawn up and sent to the First

Lady on behalf of every organization in Canton, including the Board of Education, Canton Medical Society, and the Democratic Committee.

Then began the President's seven-day fight for his life. Telegrams flew across the wire giving an update on his condition. At first, it looked like he was going to be all right. On Saturday, his condition was satisfactory. McKinley's personal friends came to Buffalo from every corner of the country, including Marc Hanna, William R. Day, and George B. Frease. Ida's sister Mary Barber came immediately. There was hope on Sunday, and the attending physicians told Vice President Roosevelt he could inform the public that the President would recover. By Monday he was talking, and his wounds had closed sufficiently. On Tuesday it was universally believed that McKinley would live. Almost all of the friends who had gathered in Buffalo began returning home.

His stitches were removed on Wednesday, and his condition continued to improve. Thursday was his best day yet. He asked for a cigar, and he wanted food. He had been on a strict liquid diet since the surgery. He had no pain and was in good spirits. On Friday the President took a sudden turn for the worse. Evidently the food had not digested properly and he was growing weaker. Mrs. Barber "hastily returned from Canton" to be with her sister. By Friday afternoon, McKinley knew he was going to die. He called all of the surgeons to his bedside and said, "It is useless gentlemen. I think we ought to have prayer." The room grew quiet, and emotions ran high. He asked for his wife.

When Ida came into the room, he kissed her. Then he looked up and said faintly, "Good bye—Goodbye all. . . . It is God's way. His will, not ours, be done." And he was gone. It was 2:15 a.m. on Saturday, September 14.

Within seven minutes news of the President's death reached *The Repository* newsroom by wire. Seven minutes later, the press was running a special edition, bordered in black. The newspaper staff gave the signal to ring the bell, informing Canton that their favorite son was dead. Roosevelt had gone back to his camp in the Adirondacks in New York. He arrived in Buffalo Saturday morning and took the Oath of Office in the Milburn residence.

An autopsy revealed that the holes had been perfectly closed by the stitches, but the tissue around each hole had become gangrened. The bullet had passed through the stomach and into the back walls of the abdomen, tearing the upper part of the kidney. The track of the bullet was also gangrened. There was no sign of disease in any of the other organs. The doctors were surprised to find the gangrene, suggesting the possibility that the bullet had been poisoned. To this day, there is no explanation for it.

The assassin's trial took only two days. The jury took less than an hour to convict him. He was sent to Auburn State Prison, where he died in the electric chair on October 29, 1901.

CANTON

Funeral arrangements began immediately following the President's death. His body was to lay in state at Buffalo and Washington, D.C. before coming home to Canton. Internment would be at the West Lawn Cemetery. Brief services were held in Buffalo at the Milburn home. Mrs. McKinley stayed at the top of the stairs where she could see and hear the service. Afterwards, the body was taken to City Hall, escorted by the military, where an estimated 100,000 passed through to see him.

Back in Canton, an informal service was organized at the Methodist Church right after news arrived. A *Repository* editorial on that day read, in part:

> Unspeakable anguish on every face; eyes that tell of tears; hearts that throb as if to break; the rush of emotion that surges up in unbidden storm—evidences of these and myriad more, tell but little of the chilling grief that has the people in its cruel grasp. Memory is the dearest friend now. Bright and beautiful and inspiring, it glows with tenderest, dearest, recollection of him for whom millions mourn, as man was never mourned by man. Husband, father, soldier, statesman, friend—none can too gloriously paint the picture for the wisest and best American manhood was typified in William McKinley.

Most of the stores changed their newspaper ads to read simply, "In Memoriam," bordered in black. Charles Dougherty, the county recorder, decorated his home in the same black crepe that had been used when Presidents Lincoln and Garfield had been assassinated. Both the Grand Army Band and Thayer's Military Band offered to be part of the funeral parade.

On Monday morning at 8:37, the train carrying the President's body left Buffalo for Washington, D.C. The 420-mile trip was a "continuous pageant of mourning," as town after town bands played and choirs sang as the train went by. "Nearer My God to Thee," which had become known as the President's hymn, was heard throughout the trip. At 9:30 Tuesday morning the funeral procession traveled down Pennsylvania Avenue toward the Capitol. At 10:45 the casket was carried into the rotunda, and the public was admitted at noon. The doors closed at 7:30 that evening. The body was then brought to the railroad station, escorted by the U.S. Cavalry, and placed on the train for Canton.

Every building except the McKinley residence was draped in black when the train arrived in town at 11:08 Wednesday morning. Every church bell in the county rang out as the train passed. The McKinley arch had been reconstructed and placed at Sixth and Market, where it had stood during the Front Porch Campaign. This time, there were four other arches placed around town, honoring the fallen President. The local chapter of the Grand Army of the Republic unanimously voted to change their name from Canton Post No. 25 to William McKinley Post No. 25 on Wednesday. Schools were closed for the rest of the week, and City Council passed a resolution that all businesses in Canton close on the day of the funeral. George B. Frease, the postmaster, received orders from Washington to close the post office Tuesday and Wednesday from 10:00 to 4:00, and all day Thursday.

Honorary pall bearers selected by the family included John C. Dueber, George B. Frease, R.A. Cassidy, William R. Day, Joseph Biechele, Henry W. Harter, William A. Lynch, and Thomas M. McCarty. An estimated 50,000 people lined the sidewalks as the procession went from the train station to the courthouse. McCrea & Arnold's hearse was drawn by four jet black horses. Roosevelt's carriage took him to the George D. Harter home, where it is said he broke down in tears when talking about McKinley. The Grand Army Band played "Nearer My God to Thee." Only two lights were burning as the body lay in state at the courthouse. According to Stark County Historian E.T. Heald, "The dim light partly concealed the countenance of the deceased President, which had become darkened and discolored from the rapid progress of the infected tissue." The public was admitted to the courthouse at 1:15, where 400–500 people passed by every five minutes. Thousands were still waiting in line when the doors closed at 6:00 that evening and the body was taken to the McKinley residence.

Mrs. McKinley spent a half hour alone with the casket on Thursday morning. She stayed at home all day and did not attend any of the public services for her slain husband. At 12:30, Thayer's Military Band, Troop A, gathered at the McKinley home. The casket was covered in flowers. The funeral procession began at 1:14 and arrived at the First Methodist Church at 1:30. Roosevelt sat in the front pew. Forty Senators, 120 representatives, and many state governors attended the ceremony. The altar was blanketed in floral arrangements, some even coming from abroad.

The procession from the church to the cemetery began at 3:30. There was a brief service at the Werts receiving vault, which had been chosen as a temporary resting place for the President until a suitable memorial could be built. At 4:00, a military salute to the dead was fired by Battery A of Cleveland.

A crowd estimated at 100,000 had descended upon the city of Canton, whose population was only 30,000 at the time. After the ceremonies concluded, the railroads were kept busy all night returning people from whence they came.

On the day of the funeral, William R. Day met with a few friends to consider what should be done in the way of a memorial for the President. They visited two sites and immediately chose the hill where the McKinley National Memorial is now located. Ironically, McKinley had often remarked that the hill would make an ideal spot for a memorial tribute to Stark County's war veterans.

The McKinley National Memorial Association was formally organized on September 26, 1901 for the sole purpose of erecting and maintaining a memorial to the 25th president of the United States, William McKinley. The association issued an appeal for funds on October 10, 1901. Ohio Governor George K. Nash issued a proclamation asking that January 29, 1902, the President's birthday, be observed by schoolchildren, and that every child should be given an opportunity to contribute to the Memorial Fund. So it was that thousands of dollars were raised from the "pennies of schoolchildren."

The association acquired 26 acres of land from the Cemetery Association and adjacent property owners. By June 1903, $500,000 had been raised, so the association began taking design submissions. They received over 60. New Yorker Harold Van Buren Magonigle's design was chosen.

From the air, the design combines the cross of a martyred President with the sword of the commander-in-chief during a time of war. The monument itself is at the center of the cross, and forms the handle of the sword. The reflecting pool known as the Long Water, which was removed in the 1950s, forms the blade of the sword. The Long Water was made up of five levels, each 20 inches higher than the one before it, forming four cascades. It was 575 feet long. Maintenance of the Long Water proved to be both time consuming and never-ending. A *Repository* article in 1947 said, "Designed as one of the main scenic features of the monument surroundings, the pool has been an eyesore for years." Instead of peacefully cascading, the water was often stagnant. So it was filled in, forming the grassy basin it is today.

The first shovel of dirt was turned on June 6, 1905. Harrison Granite Company of New York built the mausoleum and approaches, while Gorham Manufacturing Company did the bronze work on the dome, doors, cornices, and interior. The cornerstone was laid on November 16, 1905. Mrs. McKinley and her family were present, and William R. Day led the ceremony. Information about McKinley's life was placed into the cornerstone.

The dedication of the memorial was scheduled for September 30, 1907. Sadly, Mrs. McKinley died earlier that year, so she was not able to see the ceremonies honoring her fallen husband. Roosevelt gave the keynote address and presided over the reviewing stand for the parade through Public Square. There were seats for 3,000 along the steps of the Memorial, with some seats reserved for the 23rd OVI, McKinley's Civil War regiment.

The memorial was a thing of beauty and remains a crown jewel of Canton to this day. A bronze statue of McKinley stands halfway up the 108 granite steps, sculpted by Charles Henry Niehaus, a native of Canton. It was modeled after a photo taken of the President by Francis B. Johnston in Buffalo, just a few hours before he was shot. He holds a manuscript of his last speech in his hand, and his chair is draped in ivy—a symbol of constancy, which was one of McKinley's most eminent traits. The statue was unveiled by Miss Helen McKinley, the President's sister.

What the public did not know on the day of the dedication was the bodies of McKinley and his family had not yet been placed in the mausoleum. They were moved from the Werts receiving vault on October 10, 1907. The bodies of the children were exhumed and moved on the same day.

The association had raised $37,000 more than the construction costs in order to set up an endowment for the memorial's maintenance. By 1928, the money was almost completely gone. H.H. Timken, Ed Langenbach, and Paul B. Belden secured an additional $106,000 for the endowment. Ten years later, operating expenses were far exceeding any income generated from investments and the sale of souvenirs. Meanwhile, maintenance needs continued to accumulate. In 1939, the association tried to make the local memorial into a National Monument. They met with the National Park Service, but they weren't interested. In 1940 a bill was introduced in Congress authorizing $100,000 for needed repairs to the memorial. Unfortunately, with World War II looming on the horizon, Congress was more concerned with spending money on defense. In 1943, the memorial was turned over to the Ohio State Archeological and Historical Society (now the Ohio Historical Society), who ran it like an absentee landlord. In 1964, a $73,000 grant from the Timken Foundation funded much needed repairs for the memorial.

Ownership of the McKinley National Memorial was officially transferred to the Stark County Historical Society (now the McKinley Museum) in 1972. As part of the agreement, "The tomb structure and grounds shall be kept open without charge to the general public." Today, the memorial continues to be privately owned by the McKinley Museum. Income for repairs and maintenance is generated from federal grants for specific projects. For almost a century, the memorial has remained as a testament to the life and career of William McKinley, Canton's favorite son and America's beloved 25th President.

Chapter Four

"THE CITY OF DIVERSIFIED INDUSTRIES"

Canton in the Victorian era exemplified the romantic nostalgia of the past. Market Street was lined with cobblestone. A fountain cascaded in the breeze in the courthouse yard on Public Square. The streetlights were still lit by a lamplighter. Majestic downtown residences stood in the center of vast lawns, rolling down to iron fences near the sidewalk. The main shopping center was still on East Tuscarawas Street, around Public Square, and up Market Street. Empty hitching posts were as hard to come by as parking spots in later years.

By the end of the Civil War, the pioneer era was over. The standard of living had increased dramatically, and the railroad brought more products to town at a cheaper price. Newcomers to Canton were successful men with money behind them. This new generation was entirely different from the pioneers who came before them. Merchants were selling a wide variety of products to Canton's consumers, many of whom were apparently taking advantage of "lines of credit." At William Stuart's Great Bargain House, a $25 purchase could be yours for $2 down and $1 a week or $4 a month. He sold watches, ice chests, clocks, and china. In the pioneer days, storeowners would sell supplies to customers in exchange for goods. Or they provided "store tabs" so that customers could pay at the harvest when they took their crops to market. While the installment plan encouraged people to buy things, it also meant delayed payment for the storeowner. To help ease that problem, David Zollars announced in 1870 that customers would save 8–20 percent if they paid with cash. He was selling muslin, wool serges, and "prime Irish poplin" for 8, 10, and 40¢ a yard.

There were many merchants advertising their products in the postwar period. J.B. McCrea manufactured furniture, mirrors, window shades, upholstery, and mattresses. Raynolds & Saxton sold guns, paints, oils, meats, rugs, vanilla, window cornices, picture frames, buggy springs, oil cloth, putty, and road scrapers. I.P. Mill sold ready-made clothing, which greatly upset Canton's tailors. He was selling overcoats for $5–10 and hats and caps for a mere 50¢ to $1. E.D. Keplinger sold kid gloves, dry goods, silks, and hosiery. H. Gottshall's Excelsior Meat Market had two meat wagons that made free deliveries inside the city limits three times a week. McCrea's was selling haircloth sofas, chairs, and tables trimmed in the popular Victorian gingerbread designs. Tall carved beds, high dressers with mirrors, and floral Brussels carpets could all be found in his store.

Advertising in *The Repository* became increasingly important as merchants competed for a slice of the market. In 1866, the newspaper acquired a Potter cylinder steam power press with new typefaces and was more than adequately equipped to handle the blossoming advertising industry. Canton's citizens had money to spend, and they were becoming discriminating shoppers. More newspaper ads appeared, each with better claims than the last one. J.L. Arnold & Co. called themselves the "leading furniture house in Stark County." Before 1869, Deuble's Jewelry rarely advertised in the newspaper. When their first ad appeared on June 3, 1869, it ran unchanged for an entire year. It was a two-column ad, 2 inches high, and was so packed with information, readers needed a magnifying glass to decipher the tiny type! They advertised themselves as the "Old & Reliable Jewelry Establishment, at the old and well known place on the East Side of Public Square." The ad went on to say, "we are enabled to sell cheaper than any others because we buy for cash and pay no high rents." They also advertised pianos, melodeons, guitars, violins, fifes, chinaware, and toys.

Stern & Mann, Canton's legendary department store, opened its doors in 1887. Max Stern and Henry Mann were living in two different states before forming a partnership and moving to Canton. Stern operated a store with his father in Easton, Pennsylvania, and Mann was in business for himself in Elizabethtown, New York. A mutual friend told them Canton was a blossoming young town with a population of 23,000 and climbing. What was even better, he told them, there was a business similar to the stores they were running that could be bought for a song. Stern and Mann, who were brothers-in-law, discussed the opportunity and decided a visit to Canton was in order.

Mann came to Canton and liked what he saw. He bought Winterhalter Millinery Store on South Market Avenue for $5,700 and rechristened it Stern & Mann. The store originally employed six people and sold mostly hats. But they also stocked ribbons, buttons, fabric, and some dressmaking supplies. The clerks were stationed behind the counters and did not roam the floor helping customers. The store opened at 7:00 a.m. and stayed open until the last customer left at night, which was usually around 9:00 during the week. But on Saturday night, the store was open until after midnight!

In those days, Stern & Mann extended credit to those "known to be reliable." Their 1890s equivalent of modern day department store plastic was a row of nails on the wall. The customer's name and amount owed was written on a piece of brown wrapping paper, torn off the roll, and stuck on one of the nails. When the bill was settled, the note came down.

CANTON

Since the pioneer days, women had always made their own clothes. Those with more disposable income bought fabric and took it to a dressmaker for a custom fit. In addition to fabric, a woman went to the store to buy things she couldn't make herself, like hats, fancy goods, and "notions." Stern & Mann provided anything the modern woman could possibly want.

As the store grew, Stern & Mann occupied several different buildings over the years. In 1902, they moved to North Market Avenue and Second Street, as Canton's commercial district migrated north of Public Square. At that time, they expanded to employ 40 workers. Ten years later the store moved further north on Market Avenue. The second generation entered the business in the 1910s. They were at the helm during the 1925 expansion when the store moved to a 48,000 square foot building at 301 West Tuscarawas Street, employing nearly 200 people.

Other clothing retailers were also operating in Canton during this time. The Union Clothing Manufacturing Company was selling $20 and $25 tailor-made suits for $15. When the company folded in 1892, C.N. Vicary was appointed the liquidation administrator and came to Canton from LeRoy, New York with his partner L.W. Steuber. Vicary and Steuber opened a shop on Market Avenue next to Stern & Mann. During the Panic of 1892, Steuber returned to LeRoy and left Vicary to carry on alone. Vicary acquired Union's stock of clothing at a cheap rate and started the Vicary Union Store. He too offered an attractive installment plan to encourage business.

In the 1870s, John Danner was hard at work manufacturing his patented revolving bookcase. He was one of the first native born Cantonians. His father had come to town in 1816 and married Anna Slusser, daughter of mill builder Philip Slusser, in 1821. There were no public schools yet, so young John went to a private school. Danner started the Canton Stove Works in 1865 with John R. Bucher but sold out after a year. Then he went into the clothing and dry goods business. But the soul of an inventor was burning inside of him. He had dreams of a revolutionary bookcase design and began experimenting with different concepts. He settled on the pivot and post design and obtained a patent in 1874. He then sold his dry goods business to focus exclusively on his bookcases.

And were they ever popular! Orders came in faster than he could fill them. He started the John Danner Revolving Bookcase Company and set up a factory in the back of his farmhouse at Market and Fifth Street for 40 employees. Before long, prominent names appeared on his customer list. In 1877 Yale College ordered one. The following year he exhibited his bookcases at the Paris International Exhibition and won a gold medal. In 1880, Danner was shipping bookcases across the country and around the world, selling over 6,000. His customers were predominantly public offices, lawyers, clergy, physicians, businessmen, libraries, courts, reading rooms, and literary and musical societies. The bookcases could be ordered in oak, black walnut, western ash, and Philippino mahogany.

In the 1880s, Danner added a line of revolving store and restaurant stools, as well as other kinds of goods cases. He had to move to a bigger facility twice in order to accommodate expanding sales. He employed 150 skilled workers. Later he added office cases, cabinets for the home, book racks, and hanging mirrors. Several orders from czarist Russia kept the company busy through the Panic of 1893. Then tragedy struck. On May 31, 1903, a fire of unknown origin swept through the factory, completely destroying the entire plant in three hours. The heat was so intense it actually melted the fire hoses. It was a tremendous loss for him, estimated at $100,000. Danner's insurance only covered $40,000. He was 80 years old at the time. Adding to the loss, many of the workers owned their own tools and kept them at the factory.

Despite the hardship, Danner rebuilt his factory bigger than before. He continued operation for another 13 years but never fully recovered from the fire. The company was liquidated in 1916. Danner had seven kids and was a staunch Prohibitionist. Though he enjoyed fame for his bookcases, he is perhaps best known locally for his seminal work *Old Landmarks of Canton and Stark County*. He regularly published his reminiscences, which are invaluable historical resources—in his lifetime, Danner saw Canton grow from a town of 700 to a city of 85,000.

In the post–Civil War period, many of the industries Canton has become known for were starting up or moving to town. Belden Brick, Hoover, Timken, Diebold, and Dueber-Hampden are just a few of the major businesses that helped Canton earn the title of "The City of Diversified Industries."

Though the first brickyard in the area was established just east of Canton in 1813, the brick industry really began in the postwar era when Henry S. Belden got a sore throat. By the age of 32, Belden had already served as Canton's mayor and had a successful private law practice. He became sick with a sore throat and moved to his father's farm near Waco, Ohio, hoping the fresh air would restore his health. But Belden was too active to sit around recuperating. He discovered coal deposits on the farm and opened a mining operation that led to the unearthing of fire clay and shale deposits. Belden went to the 1876 Centennial Fair in Philadelphia and saw a stiff-mud brick making machine. He came home and founded the Canton Brick Company to make paving bricks at the Belden Farm. Others had attempted to make a paving brick, but no one had succeeded in doing so.

Belden received a contract to pave a block of Cherry Street between Tuscarawas Street and Second Street SE. The city liked what it saw, and soon Belden was paving other city streets, including the well traveled area of Public Square.

CANTON

As Belden developed his revolutionary brick, another local company was about to transform the way we cleaned our homes, raising the standard of cleanliness for generations to come. In the late nineteenth century, Daniel Hoover was running a tannery on a "toll system." If a farmer brought him three hides, he would keep one for tanning the other two. In 1870, his sons bought out their father and started running the business themselves. In 1875 they started making horse collars. Farmers could drive up and have custom collars made. William, one of Daniel's sons, would also travel around the countryside selling them. It was a successful venture, but with the invention of the automobile, the demand for leather goods was waning. Hoover was looking for a way to diversify his business.

Enter Murray Spangler. He had fallen on some hard times and was working as a night janitor to make ends meet. He was asthmatic, an occupational hazard for someone who cleans for a living. Using his broom handle, a tin soap box, a fan, and a pillow case, he fabricated a machine that pulled the dust away from him. He realized the potential of his invention immediately and began looking for financial backing.

Spangler's cousin happened to be Susan Hoover, wife of William "Boss" Hoover, who was looking for new business opportunities. Spangler persuaded her to try the "suction sweeper" in her home, and she was hooked from the beginning. She told her husband about her cousin's invention, and he bought the patent from Spangler in 1908. Before long, they were manufacturing sweepers in a corner of the leather goods shop.

Business was slow at first. The cost of a vacuum cleaner was high, and few people had electricity. To help boost sales, Boss Hoover ran an ad in the *Saturday Evening Post* offering a free 10-day trial to anyone who sent in a request. Using his business ingenuity, Hoover contacted stores throughout the country and asked them to deliver the vacuum to the potential customer. And he offered the store a commission on each sale. Then he extended an offer to the store to become a Hoover dealer. Business boomed, and Hoover quickly became a household name across the country. By 1919, the horse collar and saddlery part of the business closed, and the company focused exclusively on vacuum cleaners.

Like Hoover, Henry Timken's beginnings were also in the horse transportation industry, making bearings for wagons and carriages. With the invention of the automobile, he too saw a need to refocus his business on something else. Instead of changing industries entirely, Timken sought to become a part of the blossoming automotive age.

It all began in 1865 when, after serving three years as captain of the 13th Missouri Regiment in the Civil War, Henry Timken re-started his carriage business in St. Louis. To make his carriages more comfortable, Timken invented an improved buggy spring.

"The City of Diversified Industries"

He became obsessed with making a passenger's ride as smooth as possible and was soon experimenting with the problems of strain and friction. He invented a cross-spring that won an award at the World's Columbian Exposition in Chicago in 1893.

Together with his sons William and Henry, Timken began working on an idea to improve ball bearings and roller bearings. The men wanted a showy testimony to the benefits of their new invention, so they staged a demonstration. They loaded a large wagon with hay and hitched up two very small mules. They had the mules pull the overburdened wagon up and down the street in front of City Hall. After several trips back and forth, the driver was arrested and charged with animal cruelty. One of the Timkens showed up at court and demonstrated for the judge how easy it was to pull a heavy load with their newly invented bearings. The case was dismissed.

By the turn of the century, the bearing business was so successful the company was looking to expand. St. Louis was far from the steel industry, and freight charges were still quite high in those days. Timken was impressed with the possibilities of the blossoming young auto industry, which was then centered around Cleveland, Toledo, and Detroit. As early as 1895, he had equipped several of the new-fangled "horseless carriages" with bearings. He had even won second prize in the first "horseless carriage" race in the United States. The automobile with Timken bearings had made the 53-mile race in just 10 hours and 23 minutes.

Knowing what Timken could bring to town, the Board of Trade sent President Charles A. Dougherty to St. Louis to make a pitch for Canton as the new home for Timken. On September 23, 1901, the Timkens bought five lots on Dueber Avenue and 20th Street SW. By 1902, production began in Canton with 25 employees. In 1904 the business was expanding so rapidly, new buildings were required and the workforce doubled. Within a few years, more than half of the participants in the Automobile Show at Madison Square Garden in New York City were equipped with Timken bearings.

Plenty of other famous companies were also moving to Canton during the last quarter of the nineteenth century. Diebold & Kienzle had opened a new plant to manufacture safes on July 4, 1872 in Cincinnati. The great Chicago Fire on October 8, 1871 had made Diebold a household name. When the flames were finally put out and the smoke cleared, in the ruins of the fire stood 878 safes—intact, with the papers inside unharmed.

A flood of orders rushed into the plant, and the company began to look for a place to expand their operations. They chose Canton, for both its proximity to the steel industry and location near the railroads. From Cincinnati came 150 men, and the company hired 100 locals. In addition to bank, store, office, and house safes, Diebold also produced bank vaults, steel linings, safe deposit boxes, and lockers.

CANTON

Even through the Panic of 1873, orders kept streaming in. But by 1876, the company was having trouble paying their bills. A joint stock company formed to purchase the plant and keep it from moving to Chicago. The new corporation was renamed the Diebold Safe and Lock Company. Lewis C. Bockius became a large shareholder, which allowed the company to stay in Canton.

Dueber-Hampden was yet another company that moved to Canton in the late nineteenth century. In 1885 German immigrant John C. Dueber, who manufactured high quality watch cases, had just purchased the Hampden Company, makers of watch movements. He planned to move the combined companies to the first town that would raise $100,000 to help him build a new plant. In those days, that was an astronomical sum of money. But the new company would bring with it skilled workers and their families, with the potential to increase a city's population by over 7,500!

Canton wanted to be the new home of Dueber-Hampden, and city leaders set out to make that happen. Charles A. Dougherty, a real estate dealer, closed his office and devoted his time to raising the money needed to bring the innovative watch company to town. Within three months Dougherty convinced 20 local businesses to give $5,000 each in written guarantees.

As secretary of the Board of Trade, Louis Schaefer, founder of the Opera House, met with Dueber to brag about all the advantages Canton had to offer. Based on Dougherty's written promises, the bank advanced the total sum of $100,000. The Meyers family sweetened the deal by donating 20 acres of land to build the new factory. City leaders invited Dueber and 40 associates to a meeting in Canton in June 1886. Dueber was convinced, and construction began four months later.

Dueber-Hampden needed two separate buildings—one for the case works and one for the movement factory. His innovative new company was designed to produce the finest watches in the most efficient way possible. When the complex was completed in 1888, two special charter trains brought the first 400 employees from the company's former home in Springfield, Massachusetts. The addition of so many skilled workers changed the character of Canton. The discriminating wives of watchmakers were used to a higher quality of fabric for their dresses. Stern & Mann recognized this and began stocking finer fabrics right away.

Dueber-Hampden produced some of the finest quality timepieces ever made. They pioneered the 17-jewel movement, which they combined with 14-karat gold filled cases. In 1898 they were the first to introduce the 23-jewel movement. Their signature feature was the elaborately detailed engraving on the watch case. The production was so complicated and precise that when an order was placed, the first watch was not finished for eight months. Each watch went through 480 rigorous operations before it was allowed to leave the factory.

"The City of Diversified Industries"

Dueber's success was as much from being a shrewd businessman as from being frugal. Shortly after moving to Canton, it came to his attention that $120,000 worth of gold, silver, copper, and other precious metals were lost each year as a normal part of the watchmaking process. As the cases were engraved or polished, minute particles of metal fell to the floor, stuck to walls, or became embedded in workers' clothing. Dueber decided this was not an unavoidable result of production and devised a plan to recoup some of his loss. Every night the floor was swept, and the dirt and dust was sent to the smelting department. All of the clothing workers wore—aprons, towels, overalls—were washed at the company. The laundry water was sent to a holding tank in the basement and the water was repeatedly filtered to trap wayward metal particles.

Even with its amazing success, Dueber-Hampden was not without its setbacks. Just after the company came to Canton, a ruthless cyclone swept through from the southwest and tore down the southern wing of one of the company's buildings in 1888. The wing was 230 feet long by 30 feet wide and 3 stories high. An article in *The Repository* that day said "when the building fell a crash sounding like a deep roll of thunder followed that despite the roar of the storm was heard in the heart of the city."

John Dueber died in 1907. At the time of his death, his company employed 3,000 workers, almost evenly divided between women and men. His company had become the most widely known and respected watch company in the world. It was so popular, in fact, a Dueber-Hampden watch was once used to identify a body. On October 15, 1915, a body washed up on the coast of Ireland. The *Lusitania* had been struck by a torpedo from a German U-boat and sank in May of that year, and the man was presumed to be a victim of that tragedy. But he had no identification on him– except a Dueber-Hampden pocket watch. Cunard Line officials were able to trace the man's identity by contacting Dueber Hampden in Canton. They were able to tell them who purchased the watch with the number 3,039,347.

John Dueber's son Albert took over the family business after his father's death, but he was not the astute businessman his father had been. The plants had grown old and the equipment that had once been state-of-the-art was now outdated. The company limped along, losing sales year after year. Albert finally sold the company to a group of Cleveland businessmen in September 1925 for a little more than $1.5 million. The new owners had no experience in the watchmaking business and no background in design, manufacture, or sales.

They kept the business going until the late 1920s when all of the machinery and tools were sold to Amtorg, a Russian buying agency. They wanted to introduce the art of watch making to the Russian people. The equipment was packed into 28 freight cars and shipped across the ocean. Twenty-one former Dueber-Hampden employees were hired to supervise the establishment of a Soviet watch factory in Moscow and train the new recruits.

The employees left Canton for Moscow on February 25, 1930. They were given apartments around the city and welcomed with a huge banquet. They were periodically entertained and even got a tour of the Kremlin. All expenses and salaries were paid by the government. They started out training 700 Russian laborers, but that number had increased to 1,600 by the time they left. Most of them lived there for a year, but a half dozen stayed for an additional six months before returning to the United States. Some tried to correspond, but the Soviet government censored every letter. Once the Iron Curtain dropped, the American watchmakers never heard from their Russian counterparts again. No one really knows what became of the factory, though Henry Fried, professor of horology at New York University, reported seeing Dueber-Hampden machinery in China in 1986. The watches remain a favorite among collectors and are unsurpassed in workmanship and quality.

Many other industries were thriving in downtown Canton at the turn of the century. Harvard Dental Company, founded in 1886 by Frank Case, was one of those success stories. Case was a lawyer turned industrialist who made enough money to build the famed "Case Mansion," which would become the home of the Canton Art Institute (now the Canton Museum of Art). The Harvard Company specialized in high-end dental furniture that was exported as far away as Australia, Africa, and South America. They built dental chairs, cabinets, mouth lamps, hot air syringes, water and spray heaters, sterilizers, and fountain cuspidors. The Weber Dental Company was founded in 1898 by Henry Weber, one of Case's former employees. The two companies operated simultaneously until they merged in 1937, after both founders had died.

Many of Canton's original large firms continued to prosper as well, with a few changes. In 1891 Lewis Gibbs left the Bucher and Gibbs Plow Company to devote his time to the Gibbs Lawn Rake Company, which he had organized with his sons Elmer and Alvin in 1884. They changed the name to Gibbs Manufacturing Company in the 1890s and expanded their product line to include knitting needles, crochet hooks, embroidery hoops, and stocking darners. The company entered the toy making business in 1896 when they began manufacturing a top that read "I Spin for McKinley." This ushered in a new era for the company that would catapult them to the forefront of the toy industry. Their moving mechanical animals and wagons were favorites and continue to be coveted treasures today.

Other smaller companies were also started in this period. The Troy Laundry and Dry Cleaning Company was founded in 1888 at 539 North Market Avenue. There were Troy Laundries all over the country, using machinery made in Troy, New York, the home of the shirt and collar industry. In 1892, Edward D. Lang began a one-man monument business, making marble and granite vaults and monuments by hand with a chisel and mallet. Pneumatic tools for lettering were not used until 1905, and shortly after that, work was done by electrically propelled compressed air chisels.

The Repository was also changing during this time to reflect the increasing needs of a growing community. In 1878, the paper became a daily, and the management was starting to change. George B. Frease came to *The Repository* in 1880, becoming a printer-reporter at the age of 19. He became a stockholder in 1885. The Saxtons still owned two-thirds interest, but Frease was leading the paper. In February 1886, the name was changed to *The Evening Repository*. The heirs of some of the Saxtons relinquished control of their stock in 1890, selling 33 shares to John C. Dueber. A Sunday edition was added in 1892. Frease obtained a controlling interest in the paper in 1895.

Frease bought the paper's first two typesetting machines in 1896. As the population of Canton increased, so did the demand for newspaper subscriptions. In 1895, the population was 30,000, and *The Repository*'s circulation was 4,566. They were not the only game in town, however. Readers in 1905, for example, had several choices. *The Repository* was printing evening, weekly, and Sunday editions. The *News-Democrat*, founded as the *Stark County Democrat* by John Bernard in 1833, also became a daily in 1878, printing morning and semi-weekly editions. The *Volks Zeitung* came out weekly and tri-weekly. The *Catholic Exponent* was published monthly. During the Front Porch Campaign, reporters from all over the country were stationed in Canton, making the city a center of national journalism.

Such burgeoning industries needed modern conveniences. The Canton Electric Light & Power Company was incorporated in 1883 by some of the most familiar and powerful names in town—James A. Saxton, George P. Harter, Cornelius Aultman, William K. Miller, and William McKinley. In the early days people used the arc lamp and the Edison light, a carbon filament incandescent lamp.

The growing city of Canton received its first telephone switch board on May 11, 1880. It was located on the third floor of the Trump Building, on the corner of West Tuscarawas Street and Court Street. At first, there were no telephone numbers. Callers simply asked for the person by name. The first subscribers to this radically new service included *The Repository*; St. Cloud Hotel; Miller & Huford's Omnibus and Hack Line; Lynch, Day & Lynch law office; First National Bank; and Schertzer & Haymaker's Livery and Feed Stable.

All of this modernization gave rise to certain morality questions that particularly troubled middle and upper class women. The temperance movement hit Canton full force in February 1874 when six ladies from the Methodist Church asked saloon keepers to stop selling alcohol. When they refused, the ladies knelt down on the saloon floor and started to pray. More women soon joined the crusade, paying daily visits to Canton's saloons.

Most other communities had organized church action against liquor in the 1860s, but the German immigrants who settled Canton were not interested in giving up their beer. The biggest temperance issue to hit Canton before the ladies started their prayer movement concerned closing the saloons on Sundays. There was a law, but it was not enforced. City officials decided to crack down on offenders in June 1868. Saloon owners responded by loading up wagons and setting up shop just outside the corporation limits. Many added gaming, card playing, and cock fighting, and patrons came home even wilder than before. There was a rise in petty crimes like horse stealing and shoplifting.

When the temperance ladies started praying to shut down the saloons, the issue split Canton down the middle. The temperance ladies met at the YMCA, and the out-spoken Louis Schaefer held anti-crusade meetings at his Opera House. Schaefer also owned *The Stark County Herald*, and he wrote an editorial slamming the temperance crusaders. He said that women who neglected their midweek work to "dress in gaudy silks and costly linen," who "gilded their ears, hands and bosoms with gold and diamond ornaments, and who by chemical compounds, transformed their complexions from a natural hue to one of fairest deception . . . such women were not worthy to prescribe rules of conduct for every day folk that honestly minded their own business."

Canton's religious community charged that Schaefer was contributing to the delinquency of young men and women with his anti-crusade sentiments. But Schaefer countered with the argument that true temperance was the "use, not abuse, of liquor." One day 15 temperance ladies tried to enter a beer garden operated by Henry Balser. When he refused to let them in, they began holding a temperance meeting on the street just outside the door. Henry and Mrs. Balser decided the sidewalk needed to be washed. Armed with buckets and brooms, they began vigorously cleaning the sidewalk. The dirty water splashed all over the dresses of the ladies knelt in prayer. The Balsers were subsequently arrested for disorderly conduct. Louis Schaefer and Seraphim Meyer defended them. William McKinley, William R. Day, and William A. Lynch led the prosecution. The crowds were so large, the trial was moved to Schaefer's Opera House. The jury could not agree, so there was no conviction. The city quickly adopted an ordinance against crusading, and a new ordinance prohibiting the sale of alcohol on Sundays and election days.

Sensationalism again visited Canton in June 1880 when the city held a triple hanging. Morale was low in the community at that time. The YMCA had just closed for lack of funds, and *The Repository* was riddled with stories of young boys frequenting saloons and houses of ill repute. Murders were all too frequent for a town of 12,000. Hotel robberies were reported almost weekly. It was in this climate that three boys aged 16 to 19 were executed in Public Square.

John Sammet was a local kid from Massillon. Gustave A. Ohr and George W. Mann were from Chicago and Kansas respectively. All three boys came from troubled backgrounds that ultimately led them astray.

Sammet's mother died when he was young, and he started reading "yellow" literature, which he said inspired him to commit minor crimes. By his own admission, this behavior led to drinking, gambling, and escalating crime. One day, Sammet stole several boxes of cigars in front of Christopher Spuhler, who was 16. Sammet was arrested and tried to get Spuhler to lie about the cigar heist. When Spuhler refused, Sammet shot him. He was convicted of murder on November 25, 1879.

Ohr's father died when he was seven, and his mother remarried. He was born in Germany, but he moved to Chicago with his family, where he began drinking and getting into trouble. He ran away from home and started stealing rides on freight trains trying to make his way to New York City. Mann was also a runaway. His mother had died when he was three, and he did not get along with his stepmother. Near Decatur, Illinois, Mann struck up an acquaintance with John Wattmough, a 50-year-old man who had a little money. He offered to help the man steal rides on trains in exchange for food. At Fort Wayne, they met up with Ohr.

As the trio made their way east, they stopped in Alliance. At 6:00 a.m., Wattmough bought cheese and crackers for breakfast and shared it with the boys. Ohr and Mann concocted a plan to knock the man out and take his money, watch, and some of his clothing. When he started coming to, they beat him again, this time quite a bit harder. He staggered to a nearby farmhouse and died within a few hours, but he did manage to tell his story first. Ohr and Mann were arrested and convicted of murder.

Judge Seraphim Meyer heard all three cases. He was a former Union Army colonel who organized and commanded a regiment in the Civil War. He was stern, but fair. Originally, Judge Meyer sentenced Ohr and Mann to hang on May 7 and Sammet on June 25. Perhaps to make more of spectacle—and an example—out of them, Ohr and Mann were given a stay until June 25 so all three would be hanged together. The judge's daughter took a special interest in Mann, visiting him nearly every day. She became infatuated with him and begged her father to spare his life. She reportedly was admitted to a mental institution after the hangings and later died there.

On the morning of June 25, 1880, the three boys ate lunch in their cells at 10:15. They were led outside shortly afterwards to a triple gallows. Three nooses hung from the beam. The sheriff sprung the trap at 11:43, and all three were pronounced dead.

CANTON

After the triple hanging, it was six years before a new generation stepped forward to reorganize the YMCA. Previously the YMCA had operated out of rented rooms, without a building of its own. The new organizers wanted to build Stark County's first YMCA building and were able to raise $8,020 for land. William K. Miller donated the remaining $1,000 the group needed. At a meeting at the Harter Home, $18,000 was pledged toward the cost of a new $40,000 building. There was great competition for fund raising at the time. Funds were being solicited in the community for several projects, including a new opera house, Aultman Hospital, Odd Fellows Temple, a clubhouse for the German singing societies, and a new Trinity Reformed Church building. Somehow, the YMCA raised enough funds and started to build.

Several disasters plagued the progress of the project. Just as work began in July 1889 John F. Raynolds, chair of the building committee, died. His position passed to Jacob Miller, who died the following month in August. On May 21, 1890, the walls sank 1 inch, which caused the brick and stone work to crack. Two weeks before the scheduled opening, George D. Harter (a member of the managing board and campaign committee) died. At the opening ceremonies, the new YMCA building was dedicated to Raynolds, Miller, and Harter, who had worked so hard to see it to completion.

The new YMCA provided a place for Canton's youth to participate in organized sports, some of which were brand new at the time. Charles A. Stolberg introduced basketball to the Canton YMCA on July 7, 1892, just seven months after the game was invented by G.A. Naismith, the physical director of the YMCA training college in Springfield, Massachusetts. By 1900, it was by far the most popular indoor sport in Canton. The first girls' game of basketball took place on April 6, 1900. The players wore wide bloomers and navy blue blouses with sailor collars trimmed in white. Volleyball became very popular with the business and professional men. Handball was introduced in 1902.

Originally, the new YMCA building did not have a pool. When Herman C. Blum, a former YMCA president, died on October 17, 1897, he left $1,000 unconditionally with an additional $3,000 if the YMCA matched it through fundraising. They decided to use the windfall to build a pool where the bowling alleys were. The first indoor pool in Stark County opened on September 26, 1899.

In the new building, the YMCA offered a variety of evening classes in topics like mechanical drawing, penmanship, arithmetic, bookkeeping, and French. Later they added classes in carpentry, photography, clay modeling, music, electricity, automobiling, commercial law, salesmanship, sheet metal pattern cutting, wireless telegraphy, and business. They also offered English classes for the immigrants who were coming to town to work in Canton's factories. By 1910, membership had jumped to 1,325, an increase of 800 in just three years.

"The City of Diversified Industries"

For the first 80 years of its industrial history, Canton saw very few labor problems. In fact, the contentment of Canton's workers was often used to entice new industries to town. Employers were paying as well or better than most areas of the country; in 1860 the reaper and mower companies were paying $398 a year compared to $317 in New York City and $274 in Chicago. The first local labor union, the Iron Moulders Union, was not organized until the 1870s. The Cigar Maker's Union No. 115 followed in 1885. The 1886–1887 *City Directory* lists nine unions, including blacksmiths, carpenters, garment workers, mason and bricklayers, moulders, plasterers, and steel workers.

Labor Day became an official holiday in Ohio in 1890, but the first formal observance in Canton did not happen until 1892 when a program was planned by the Trades and Labor Assembly. Men wearing the symbols of their trades and occupations marched in a parade in full uniform down East Tuscarawas Street. There were even floats displaying the various trades. Canton stone cutters were led by a stone wagon where men worked on a stone. Five thousand people participated, despite rainy weather that made the roads muddy and generally sloppy.

A similar event was held the following year. In 1893, 1,500–1,800 people went to Akron to celebrate. In 1894, the Canton Trades and Labor Assembly held a picnic in Sprankle's Woods that drew 1,200. The following year the Panic of 1893 was really being felt, so there was no celebration in Canton. The Trade and Labor Assembly disbanded in 1897, and nothing was held for the duration of the century.

When the local unions reorganized in 1901 under the name Central Labor Unions, it also rekindled the celebrations. Representatives from Canton went to Youngstown with the Grand Army Band and Thayer's Military Band. One of President McKinley's final official acts before leaving on his fateful trip to Buffalo was to give orders to raise the flag at his home in honor of Labor Day.

While labor and trades celebrated their crafts, a new form of transportation was making the morning commutes a little easier. Canton was the only city in Stark County to build up a horsecar tradition and was the first to build a system of street cars. Alliance converted horsecars to electric within four months, and Massillon never had any. But Canton's horsecars enjoyed five years of popularity, from 1884 to 1889.

Canton's citizens began to lobby for horsecars as early as 1869, when the population was only 8,000. The biggest obstacle was deciding on a route. Some thought it should run on North Market Street, and others wanted it on Cleveland Avenue. Property values would certainly increase if a streetcar line passed by. Prominent citizens lived on both streets, and neither side would budge. Finally in 1884, the city reached a compromise. The route would run up North Market Street to Sixth Street, over Sixth Street to Cleveland Avenue, and out Cleveland Avenue to

12th Street. Three other lines went out on East Tuscarawas Street to the creek, out West Tuscarawas Street to Elgin, and south on Market Street to 12th Street. On December 18, 1884, four cars were ready to go, but a snowstorm had other ideas. Men worked on clearing the tracks with shovels, picks, and brooms.

The cars were scheduled to run every 10 minutes during morning rush hour from 6:10 to 7:00 a.m., and at 20 minute intervals the rest of the day. The last car left at 10:00 p.m. Each trip took 40 minutes, and the fare was 5¢. Drivers called out the street names as they approached. At the end of the line, the horses were unhitched and taken to the other side of the car, making the back of the car become the front. All four lines met at Public Square where passengers could transfer, but they had to take the next car going their way. Each car held 18 people.

The driver stood outside on an open platform, no matter what the weather. Mrs. William D. Theobald lived at the end of the line at 1210 South Market Street. Throughout the winter she kept a pot of coffee boiling on her stove, and all the drivers had a standing invitation to come and warm themselves during their 5–10 minute wait at the end of the line.

The people of Canton used horsecars to travel around town until 1889, when all the street railways were electrified. The whir of motors replaced the clopping and neighing of horses, as the cars clacked along an overhead electric line. The horse suddenly became obsolete for travel, which caused a glut in the horse market. The new electrified street cars were wildly popular. The lines criss-crossed city streets and the "interurbans" had regular routes to Massillon, Uhrichsville, Akron, Cleveland, Alliance, and Salem.

Tragedy struck on October 3, 1893 when 27 car bodies and 36 motors burned in a fire. Almost all of the Canton City Line's equipment and a large part of the interurbans were destroyed. The city immediately ordered new cars. The interurbans reached their peak in the 1920s, with 2,000 miles of intercity track. America's love affair with the automobile all but destroyed the public transportation system nationwide as road conditions improved and more people bought cars. By 1938, only 150 miles of track were actively in use.

If the transition to electric street cars marked the end of an era, then the passing of Louis Schaefer had much the same effect. When he died in November 1889, so did his Opera House. He had been the heart and soul of the place, and it couldn't survive without him. Quickly plans were made for the Grand Opera House to replace it. In just two months, $50,000 had been subscribed to build it. Architect Oscar Cobb of Chicago was chosen to design it. He had worked on 300 opera houses across the country. Cobb began work on June 18, 1890.

"The City of Diversified Industries"

The Grand Opera House went up quickly. Its grand opening was held on October 30, 1890 with a performance of the comique opera *Fauvette* by the Boston Ideal Opera Company. But it wasn't the show most of the audience, dressed in their opera best, expected to see. The Boston Ideal Opera Company had come to town before and gave a highly acclaimed performance. Marsh Barber, manager of the Grand Opera House, was thrilled to book the Boston Ideal Opera Company for another successful engagement. What he didn't know was that the group that had previously come to Canton had changed their name to The Bostonians, and a new comic opera had taken on the old name. Nevertheless, the show was a hit, though Barber took a bit of ribbing for his mistake.

The Grand Opera House was quite a place in its heyday. It had a big foyer and a tiled floor, with a stage that was said to be the largest in Ohio. The scenery raised up instead of sliding, and the curtain was a representation of Lake Como in Switzerland. Practically every surface was finished in gold and bronze, with polished brass railings and plush seats. It was lit by electricity and heated by steam.

Its most famous event was the William McKinley birthday celebration on January 27, 1903. President Theodore Roosevelt was the guest speaker. There were 457 guests who paid $15 a plate. In total, the banquet cost $7,000—a fortune for that time! The entire place was re-floored for the party. Cleveland's leading caterer, Demarest, took over the basement and converted it to a kitchen. They brought in all of the equipment they would need to cater the dinner, including ranges. Holes were cut in the floor and special stairways were built to facilitate the serving. There were 57 waiters, 12 wine pourers, 14 cooks, and 10 dishwashers.

The menu included blue points, bouillon, sweetbread patties, filet of beef and mushrooms, potatoes, peas, crème de menthe punch, roast squab, chicken salad, ice cream, cakes, coffee, and cigars. *The Repository* listed the location of every table with a name on every seat. William R. Day was the master of ceremonies. After introducing Roosevelt, the President turned to thank him, calling him "Mr. Justice William Day," an indication that Roosevelt planned to nominate him for a seat on the Supreme Court. His nomination went to the Senate on February 19 and was confirmed four days later.

The Grand Opera House hosted several spectacular performances, including *Ben Hur*, *Robin Hood*, *Peter Pan*, and *Rip Van Winkle*. The Grand also hosted more high brow operas like *Hamlet* and *Beau Brummell*. Until the new Auditorium was finished in 1904, there were no Sunday programs at the Grand, except religious ones sponsored by the YMCA or church groups. By 1915, they were doing non-religious Sunday performances.

By the 1920s, there was increased competition from radio and several motion picture houses in Canton, and the Grand Opera House was forced to follow suit or be put out of business. It hosted movies and burlesque shows, trying to hold on to a slice of the market. It struggled on for 15 years, attracting a "rough and tumble" crowd with its programming, before finally closing down. Robert E. Beck bought the property from Henry S. Belden Jr. in 1945 for $17,500. He did repairs and sold it to the Bethel Tabernacle the following year for $50,000.

Canton built the first hospital in Stark County in 1890 through the generosity of Katherine Barron Aultman, widow of Cornelius Aultman, and Elizabeth Harter, daughter of Cornelius Aultman and widow of George D. Harter. Together these two women supplied the funds to build Aultman Hospital as a memorial to Cornelius Aultman. A hospital was a novel idea in 1890, and there were very few in communities across the nation. The cornerstone was laid on September 28, 1890 in front of a crowd of thousands. It was finished in July 1891 but didn't open until January 1892. It boasted 40 rooms with steam heat. It was lit with both gas and electricity, but doctors still carried oil lamps with them from floor to floor.

The hospital had to wait almost a month for its first patient. Mrs. Catherine Meyer of 151 West Tuscarawas Street fell on an icy sidewalk and fractured her leg. The first operation was performed by Dr. James Fraunfelter on Norman L. Deuble, who sustained injuries to his head when he feel off his high wheeler bicycle. His surgeon did the best work he could, but Deuble died anyway. Despite this high profile death, the track record of the hospital was excellent for the time. Out of the 70 patients admitted within the first nine months, 30 required surgery and only 7 died.

A Ladies Auxiliary formed as soon as the hospital opened. They worked tirelessly for the hospital raising money. Donation Days were big community-wide events. The Flower Mission provided flowers to every patient on a weekly basis for over 30 years, until the Elizabeth Harter Pavilion added 100 beds in 1924 and the task became too great for the small group of aging ladies.

When the hospital first opened, patients paid $1 a day, though a private room was a bit more. There was no smoking allowed in the hospital, and no matches were permitted. The employees worked incredibly hard, with only two half-days off per month and half a Sunday when they could be spared.

Training classes began as soon as the hospital opened as well, and a class graduated every year from Aultman School of Nursing. During World War II two classes graduated annually to accommodate the extra students who would be going off to war. In 1944, another 100 beds were added when the McKinley Pavilion was built. The project was partially funded by the Timken Foundation, which gave a total of $322,350 each to Aultman Hospital and Mercy Hospital.

This is a reconstructed plat of the original 100 blocks as laid out by Canton's founder Bezaleel Wells. Based on property abstracts, it shows the original owner, date filed, and price paid for each lot. The gray lots were the ones Wells gave to the city. This version appeared in the March 31, 1940 issue of the Repository. The original plat drawn and recorded by Wells is now part of the McKinley Museum's permanent collection.

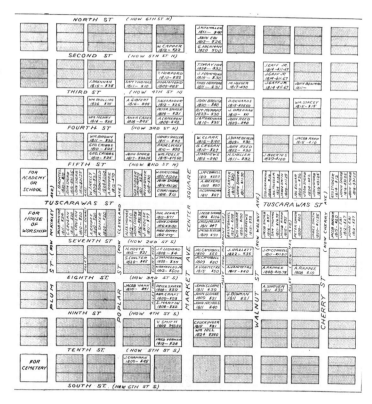

John Saxton set up his first print shop and published The Repository in his home. It was located on the southeast corner of Third Street SE and South Market Avenue, where the McKinley Hotel later stood. His son, Joseph Saxton, wrote the following on the back of the photo: "The home in which I was born October 7, 1829."

Joshua Gibbs patented the bar share plow in 1836. His son Lewis later patented the Imperial Plow, manufactured by Bucher, Gibbs & Company.

Grand Army of the Republic member Thomas R. Kirk poses with his cornet on September 20, 1870. The Grand Army Band was organized in 1866, 13 years before the local GAR post was established. Though it was not directly affiliated with the GAR, a core group of Civil War veterans were charter members.

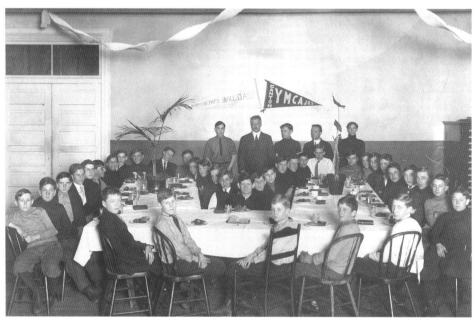

Founded in 1866, the Canton branch of the YMCA became a social center for the town's young men. The Business Boys Bible Class and Canton YMCA Juniors were some of the many clubs sponsored by the YMCA.

William McKinley is pictured here as a young Civil War soldier. He was just 18 years old when this photo was taken in 1861.

Ida Saxton was the belle of Canton when she married William McKinley, a dashing young lawyer who had recently moved to town.

President McKinley poses on "Women's Day" during the 1896 Front Porch Campaign. Though women would not be able to vote until the 19th Amendment was ratified in 1920, McKinley courted them like any other political group. It was believed that although they could not cast a vote themselves, they would be able to influence the votes of their husbands.

During McKinley's 1896 Front Porch Campaign, a massive arch was constructed at the intersection of Sixth Street and Market Avenue. After the assassination, the arch was rebuilt and several others were added around town.

William McKinley casting his vote in the 1896 campaign. He voted in Canton at Precinct B of the First Ward at 8:55 a.m. with his brother Abner and Sam Saxton.

Judge William R. Day in his study at his home on North Market Avenue. Day was one of McKinley's greatest supporters. He went on to earn a nomination to the Supreme Court from President Theodore Roosevelt, McKinley's second vice president.

167

RECEIVED at   27 H RB NR 73 paid Govt   43oP M/

Buffalo NY Sep 8-19ol
                    Geo B Frease.
                                canton .6
The Following Bulletin was issued by the Presidents Physicians
at 4 pm . The President since the last Bulletin has slept
quetly four hours. altogether since nine oclock his condition
is satisfactory to all the Physicians present. Pulse 128
Temperature lol Respiration 28 .
                        Sined P M Rixey MD
            Mann Roswell Park Herman Mynter Eugene Wasdin
                        Charles McBurney.
                        Geo B Coretelyou Secy.
                        To The President.

Early reports were optimistic, suggesting that the President would recover from his wounds. His doctors were shocked when he took a turn for the worse a few days later.

A catastrophic fire swept through the Danner Revolving Bookcase Company in May 1903. The heat was so intense it actually melted the fire hoses. It was a tremendous loss for John Danner, estimated at $100,000. His insurance only covered $40,000. Danner was 80 years old at the time.

President Roosevelt, Mayor Turnbull, and Governor Harris review the dedication parade from the President's stand at Public Square, September 30, 1907.

The first Hoover vacuum cleaners appeared in 1908.

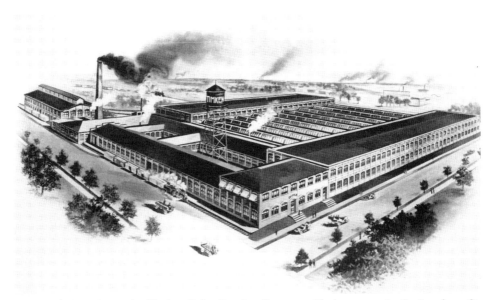

An aerial view shows the Timken Roller Bearing Company. Timken came to Canton from St. Louis in 1901 to be closer to the auto and steel industries, which were centered around Cleveland, Toledo, and Detroit.

By 1919, the original horse collar and saddlery part of the Hoover Company closed and the business began to focus exclusively on vacuum cleaners. This photo of the factory was taken in the 1920s.

Diebold officials pose with a safe, c. 1870. After the Great Chicago Fire on October 8, 1871, Diebold safes were among the few things still standing in the rubble. The company moved to Canton shortly afterwards. The officials are as follows, from left to right: (front row) Carl Diebold, John W. Norris, Jacob Kienzle, J.C. Hintz, (back row) Theodore Pierong, Frederick Baehrens, Oliver E. Converse, George W. Clark, and Andrew Paar.

A large Dueber-Hampden pocket watch float was a highlight of Canton's Fourth of July parade in 1900.

The reverse of this undated photo reads, "Another Tallyho party in Canton."

The imposing Case mansion stands on a hill in the background of this early motoring scene. The expansive home was built by Frank Case, founder of the Harvard Dental Chair Company. The mansion later became the home of the Canton Art Institute, now known as the Canton Museum of Art.

Known as the "interurban," the Canton-Massillon Electric Railway started out with horse cars in 1884. By 1890, the cars were completely electrified. This photo was taken c. 1900.

This is the interior of the Grand Opera House, 1892. The most famous event held there was the William McKinley birthday celebration on January 27, 1903. President Theodore Roosevelt was the guest speaker.

Aultman Memorial Hospital, the first hospital in Stark County, was built in 1890.

The 1899 graduates of the Aultman School of Nursing pose here. Training classes for nursing began as soon as the hospital opened.

Strolling on the promenade was a favorite leisure activity at Meyers Lake in 1905.

In 1907, a balloon cost $1,000. Through contributions, the Aero Club was able to raise enough money to buy one, which they named "The Ohio." When it was not in use, it was deflated and stored in the basement of the Courtland Hotel. Other balloons that flew out of Canton included "The Sky Pilot," "The Buckeye," "Cleveland," "All America," and "You and I."

The Aero Club prepares to launch their balloon "The Sky Pilot."

William Martin's monoplane was known as The Martin Glider. When he invented it in 1909, it was the first of its kind in the world.

The Alhambra theater advertised The Climbers *September 1915. An advertisement in* The Repository *for the show described it as "from the famous play by the same name by Clyde Finch." Prices were 5 and 10¢ for a matinee, and all evening seats were 10¢. It was being shown for three days—September 7, 8, and 9.*

A car with live bears advertises the "Hippodrome" at the Auditorium that evening.

The Barnum Bailey Circus came to town on May 25, 1904 and paraded down South Market Avenue.

Founded by John Saxton in 1815, The Repository is one of the oldest newspapers in Ohio. The editor and staff are shown here around the turn of the twentieth century. H Frease is standing.

A 1918 parade through downtown Canton features in the background the famous "largest flag in all the world." It was made by the women of Canton to help sell Liberty Bonds during World War I. The flag was 53 feet tall and 120 feet wide.

THIS
PROPERTY
PROTECTED
═ BY THE ═
CANTON
HOME
GUARD

Homes around town posted signs like this one, indicating they were protected by the Canton Home Guard.

A World War I band from Canton poses for a photograph. Generally speaking, soldiers stayed in groups from their hometowns in World War I, a practice that would change in World War II.

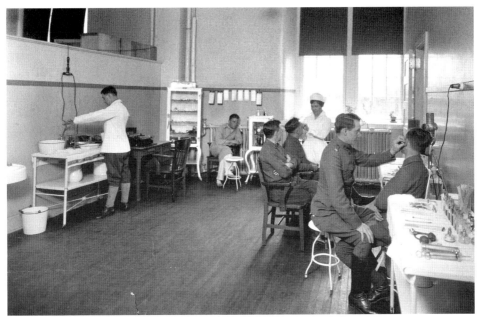

World War I soldiers are tended to at Mercy Hospital.

Football star Jim Thorpe led the Canton Bulldogs to a 1919 World Championship. Thorpe also competed in the 1912 Olympics in the decathlon and pentathlon, track and field's most grueling events.

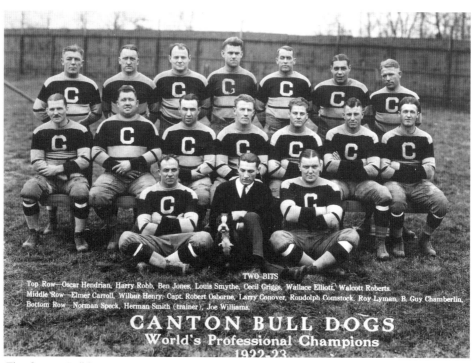

TWO BITS

Top Row—Oscar Hendrian, Harry Robb, Ben Jones, Louis Smythe, Cecil Griggs, Wallace Elliott, Walcott Roberts.
Middle Row—Elmer Carroll, Wilbur Henry, Capt. Robert Osborne, Larry Conover, Roudolph Comstock, Roy Lyman, B. Guy Chamberlin.
Bottom Row—Norman Speck, Herman Smith (trainer), Joe Williams.

CANTON BULL DOGS
World's Professional Champions
1922-23

The Canton Bulldogs were the 1922–1923 World Professional Champions.

In 1930 Timken ordered a steam locomotive and christened it Timken 1111—known as The Four Aces. It was the first steam locomotive completely equipped with Timken roller bearings.

The grand lobby of the George D. Harter Bank was a highlight of the architecture in downtown Canton in the 1920s.

Don R. Mellett, *editor of the*
Canton Daily News, *was gunned
down in his driveway on July
17,1926 by underworld bosses
for exposing crime and corruption
in the pages of his newspaper.*

*McCrory's was one of the most popular stores in the 1940s. Downtown was the heart of the
shopping district until the growing suburbs started pulling stores into Canton's many
strip malls.*

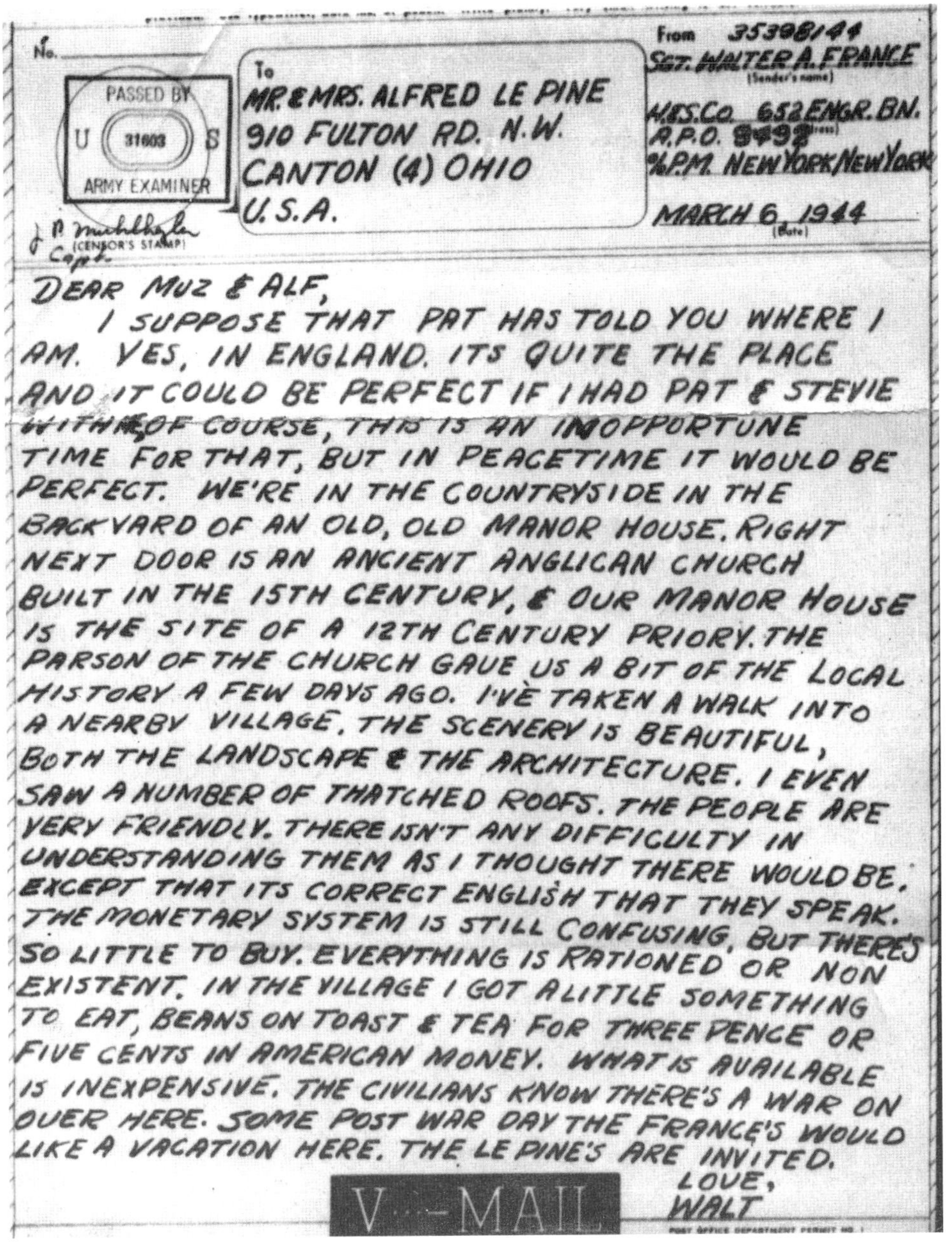

No.

PASSED BY
U 31603 S
ARMY EXAMINER

J. P. Muhlhofer Capt.
(CENSOR'S STAMP)

To
MR. & MRS. ALFRED LE PINE
910 FULTON RD. N.W.
CANTON (4) OHIO
U.S.A.

From 35398144
SGT. WALTER A. FRANCE
(Sender's name)
H&S Co. 652 ENGR. BN.
A.P.O. 9492
% P.M. NEW YORK, NEW YORK
MARCH 6, 1944
(Date)

DEAR MUZ & ALF,

I SUPPOSE THAT PAT HAS TOLD YOU WHERE I AM. YES, IN ENGLAND. ITS QUITE THE PLACE AND IT COULD BE PERFECT IF I HAD PAT & STEVIE WITH ME. OF COURSE, THIS IS AN INOPPORTUNE TIME FOR THAT, BUT IN PEACETIME IT WOULD BE PERFECT. WE'RE IN THE COUNTRYSIDE IN THE BACKYARD OF AN OLD, OLD MANOR HOUSE. RIGHT NEXT DOOR IS AN ANCIENT ANGLICAN CHURCH BUILT IN THE 15TH CENTURY, & OUR MANOR HOUSE IS THE SITE OF A 12TH CENTURY PRIORY. THE PARSON OF THE CHURCH GAVE US A BIT OF THE LOCAL HISTORY A FEW DAYS AGO. I'VE TAKEN A WALK INTO A NEARBY VILLAGE. THE SCENERY IS BEAUTIFUL, BOTH THE LANDSCAPE & THE ARCHITECTURE. I EVEN SAW A NUMBER OF THATCHED ROOFS. THE PEOPLE ARE VERY FRIENDLY. THERE ISN'T ANY DIFFICULTY IN UNDERSTANDING THEM AS I THOUGHT THERE WOULD BE. EXCEPT THAT ITS CORRECT ENGLISH THAT THEY SPEAK. THE MONETARY SYSTEM IS STILL CONFUSING, BUT THERE'S SO LITTLE TO BUY. EVERYTHING IS RATIONED OR NON EXISTENT. IN THE VILLAGE I GOT A LITTLE SOMETHING TO EAT, BEANS ON TOAST & TEA FOR THREE PENCE OR FIVE CENTS IN AMERICAN MONEY. WHAT IS AVAILABLE IS INEXPENSIVE. THE CIVILIANS KNOW THERE'S A WAR ON OVER HERE. SOME POST WAR DAY THE FRANCE'S WOULD LIKE A VACATION HERE. THE LE PINE'S ARE INVITED.

LOVE,
WALT

V-MAIL

POST OFFICE DEPARTMENT PERMIT NO. 1

A letter from Sergeant Walter France to Mr. and Mrs. Alfred LePine, March 6, 1944, describes life as a soldier in Europe during World War II. V-Mail, short for Victory Mail, was used as a means to decrease the weight and volume of mail sent overseas. The letter was photographed and printed on smaller paper to save space.

The Class of 1944 and 1945 of the Aultman School of Nursing included both students and nursing cadets who were leaving for World War II.

A BASIC MILEAGE RATION
UNITED STATES OF AMERICA
OFFICE OF PRICE ADMINISTRATION

F421897 AJ

Form OPA R-525 A

Margaretta Stolberg
(NAME OF REGISTERED OWNER)

1278 N. Woodland
(R. F. D. OR STREET AND NUMBER)

Canton (CITY OR POST OFFICE) *Ohio* (STATE)

11-18-42 (DATE) *347 864 12* (USE TAX STAMP No.)

M-95-8
(VEHICLE LICENSE No.)

Ohio
(STATE OF REGISTRATION)

1937
(YEAR MODEL)

Ford
(MAKE)

Tudor
(BODY TYPE)

This is a mileage ration book from World War II. Car production stopped completely in February 1942, and gas was made available to individuals according to their importance to the war effort. Drivers were given a rating—A, B, C, X, E, or T—to purchase gas. A national speed limit of 35 miles per hour was established to save gasoline.

Mary J. Weis poses as she leaves from the Pennsylvania Depot in Canton to join the Women's Army Corps (WAC) on March 4, 1943.

Canton was honored in 1953 when it was chosen as an "All-America City" by the National Municipal League and Look magazine. Mayor Carl Wise and Ralph E. Furbay, president of the Canton Chamber of Commerce, accept the award from representatives of the National Municipal League.

Tiny ballerinas pose for a photo as they rehearse for a production put on by The Player's Guild in the 1950s.

The Canton Symphony Orchestra celebrates its 25th anniversary in 1962. Michael Charry was the conductor.

The official seal of the Canton Sesquicentennial celebration featured the McKinley Monument, a well-known local landmark, and Canton's slogan "The City of Diversified Industries."

A postcard shows Akron-Canton Airport's new terminal, mid-1960s. The back reads: "The new three and one-half million dollar terminal building was dedicated June 22, 1962, accommodates approximately 200,000 air passengers and 400,000 visitors annually, and is served by four major airlines."

Belden Village Mall opened on October 1, 1970. Vicary's, a locally owned department store, was one of the original anchor stores.

Chapter Five

THE DAWN OF A NEW CENTURY

At the turn of the last century, incredible changes were just on the horizon. In a few years, horse drawn vehicles would become a quaint nod to the past as the modern automobile revolutionized our way of life. Humankind would soon take to the air, overcoming gravity and defying physics. Radio and movies would entertain us like nothing before. And our nation would test its resolve in 1917 when the United States joined the fighting in The Great War, the world's first truly international conflict.

Social life in Canton was thriving at the turn of the nineteenth century. Singing societies sprang up. The Grand Army Band and Thayer's Military Band gave regular concerts in the city parks. And a little place called Meyers Lake was enjoying its heyday.

A favorite pastime was a lazy afternoon at Meyers Lake, the crown jewel of Canton. Guests drove buggies, rode bicycles, or strolled down the beautiful Promenade. In 1885, the Lakeside Street Railway Company built a line from Public Square to Meyers Lake, providing a convenient gateway to idle away a summer afternoon. The cars were large enough to seat 35, pulled by two horses on a level track. The fare was 20¢ roundtrip. On the first Sunday run, the cars were so overloaded with people Charles R. Frazer of the Humane Society stopped the car and demanded that another horse be added to pull the heavy weight. He warned the driver would be arrested for cruelty to animals if he did not comply.

The area surrounding Meyers Lake had been used as summer retreat for centuries. Arrowheads, spear points, and other artifacts indicate the presence of Native American groups around the lake. Its clear water was certainly an attractive fishing spot then as it was in later years. After the Civil War, increasing leisure time led to an interest in recreational facilities where people could escape from the city. The first organized activity at Meyers Lake was the Eclipse Boat Club, which was started in 1869. A boat house was constructed on the north shore in 1873.

The first effort at creating a resort began in 1879 when Joseph A. Meyer, grandson of Andrew Meyer who started the wheat growing estate, built the Lake Park Hotel. It was 600 feet long and two stories high, with a 12 foot veranda. It was managed by Charles Sliker, founder of the Eclipse Boat Club. Like so many early ventures, the Lake Park Hotel burned down in 1892. It was rebuilt by the Reymann Brewing

Company as the North Park Hotel and Casino. It was then sold to the Northern Ohio Traction & Light Company, which leased it to the Lakeside Country Club in 1903.

In the 1880s, a second hotel called the Lakeview was built on the eastern shore of the lake. It was a magnificent structure, with 50 rooms and ornate lattice work porches on both floors. Edward J. Meyer owned the hotel and leased it to Frank X. Menegay.

By 1886, several attractions had been built to entertain guests. There was a roller coaster, roller skating rink, ten-pin alleys, dance floors, billiard and pool tables, boats, steam yachts, picnic grounds, a half-mile horse and bicycle track, the Canton Gun Club shooting range, and ball fields. In the 1890s, it was common for entire families to move out to Meyers Lake for the summer, living in tents or simple shacks that would be transformed into lake cottages in later years. The fathers would take the street cars into town for work each morning, while the rest of the family enjoyed the summer months away from the bustle of the city.

Meyers Lake was a favorite spot of the McKinleys, who were often seen walking the grounds. Even after his election as President, McKinley always found time to return to Canton for a respite from the stress of life in Washington. According to William Arntz, a Meyers Lake employee, the President could have been assassinated at the park in the summer of 1901. He reported seeing a man with two guns strapped on to him. When he approached the man and told him firearms were not permitted in the park, the man reportedly said "I don't pay attention to things like that." When Arntz whistled for the police, the man took off and vanished. After seeing a photo of the assassin a few months later, Arntz realized the man he had seen that summer day was Leon Czolgosz.

By the turn of the century, the Northern Ohio Traction & Light Company (NOTL) had taken over many of the smaller railways. It was common practice for these companies to buy and promote amusement parks on their routes as a way to increase business. NOTL bought Meyers Lake in 1902 and made several additions and improvements. In 1909 they added a "Figure 8" roller coaster, concessions, laughing gallery (wacky mirrors that would later become a fun house), a dance hall, and a tintype photo booth. There was also a swimming beach, bandstand, wooded walkways, hotel, restaurant, and picnic grounds that were used by many industries for company gatherings. It was not uncommon to have a company picnic attract 20,000 in a single day.

Cantonians also enjoyed their card and dance clubs at the turn of the century. Older couples joined the Entres Nous Club, a dance club with select membership that included men like John M. Danner, Harry Frease, and Lewis Zollars. They held elaborately formal dances every two weeks. Other dance clubs in Canton were The Assembly and Fin de Siecle. Card clubs played progressive whist, meeting at the homes of the club members. The hostess provided supper for six to eight couples. After eating, the men retired to smoke cigars and pipes, while the women enjoyed more conversation. Then they played more whist.

There were many musical organizations to choose from, including the Canton Church Choir, the Canton Orchestral Club, and Emerson's Orchestra. Many of the singing societies had a strong German influence. The Concordia Singing Society was named after the ship that brought German immigrants to America in 1683. According to Stark County historian E.T. Heald, "Cantonians turned out en masse on October 11, 1883 to celebrate the 200th anniversary of the day Germans first landed in America." Over 2,000 paraded. The singing societies were among the most stable social groups, appearing year after year in the city directory.

Canton had a disproportionate number of secret societies for such a small city. There were the Masons, The Knights of Pythias, the GAR, and The Improved Order of Red Men, and Daughters of Pocahontas, just to name a few. The Elks held a carnival for a week at Labor Day with booths that stretched almost a mile down Cleveland Avenue.

There were three or four skating rinks, including the Tabernacle, the Vendome, and the Metropolitan, as well as two roller skating polo clubs. Camping parties regularly went on excursions to Turkeyfoot Lake or took fishing trips to Congress Lake. Canton had a total of 125 saloons in 1900.

In 1907, Frank S. Lahm founded the Aero Club of Canton, which attracted national attention. Though the Wright brothers had already made their famous flight, the airplane as we know it was not yet mainstream. So the novel idea of traveling in the sky was indeed exciting.

Frank S. Lahm became interested in aeronautics when he read some of DaVinci's work on the subject. Lahm moved to France and lived there for 50 years, returning to the Canton area to spend summers at Turkeyfoot Lake. He joined the French Aero Club and bought his own balloon. He made over 30 balloon flights during his lifetime, the last trip when he was 83 years old! Frank S. shared his love of flying with his son Frank Purdy Lahm, a graduate of West Point and a lieutenant in the army.

On one of his summer holidays, Frank S. invited Johnson Sherrick, Zebulon Davis, Marshall C. Barber, Gordon Mather, Joseph M. Blake, and H.H. Timken to dinner at the McKinley Hotel. After the group had eaten, Frank S. stood up and announced that he had not only invited the men to enjoy the pleasure of their company. He invited them to organize the Aero Club of Ohio.

At the time, a balloon cost $1,000. Through contributions, the club was able to raise enough money to buy one, which they named "The Ohio." When it was not in use, it was deflated and stored in the basement of the Courtland Hotel. Other balloons that flew out of Canton included "The Sky Pilot," "The Buckeye," "Cleveland," "All America," and "You and I." Pilots steered the balloons from the basket by using ballast. They were always trying to make flights as long as possible, both in distance and in time. Passengers also rode in the basket, under the large bag inflated with gas. Artificial gas was the preferred fuel of the balloons, and the best place in town to launch was near a gas plant on the east side of Walnut Street, just north of the Pennsylvania Railroad.

The first flight took place on September 20, 1907 from Walnut Street. Frank S. was the pilot, with Joseph Blake and Gordon Mather as passengers. They landed at Pulaski, near New Castle, Pennsylvania. Frank P. piloted the second flight with passengers J.G. Obermier and Herbert W. Alden. Orville Wright came from Dayton to see it. The flight was scheduled for January 23, 1908, but a snowstorm postponed it to the following week. Frank P. was nearly overcome by gas while the balloon inflated and hit two buildings on Walnut Street. He went on to travel above the clouds, reaching 6,930 feet above sea level. They landed at Sandy Hill, 12 miles from Oil City, Pennsylvania. They made the 100 mile trip in just 2 hours and 15 minutes.

Once natural gas came to Canton, the artificial gas plant went out of business, leaving the Aero Club looking for a new flying field. Also, after Frank P.'s close call on the second balloon flight, members decided the Walnut Street location was too dangerous for take offs. The City Council agreed to let them use the cemetery on McKinley Avenue, the very same plot of land designated by Bezaleel Wells as a graveyard. It was largely abandoned at the time, except for two or three grave sites.

Some opposed launching balloons on that particular plot of land on the grounds that it violated the terms of Bezaleel Wells's stipulation that it forever remain a cemetery. The agreement stated that if the land he donated was used for any other purpose, ownership would revert back to his heirs. Franklin Goheen, president of Goheen Paint and Manufacturing Company, filed a suit in the Common Pleas Court to stop the balloon flights in March 1908. The court held that since the property was indeed dedicated for use as a cemetery, the City had no right to allow balloon flights to launch from that location. Otherwise, the rights to the land would indeed be forfeited to Wells's heirs.

Joseph Blake, a member of the Aero Club, began to pursue the matter of clearing the title of the cemetery land. Several prominent citizens contributed funds to complete the process, which led to investigations into the two other sites designated for a school and a house of worship. Blake contacted all of the known descendents of Bezaleel Wells, who were in such far flung locations as California, Arkansas, Pennsylvania, Missouri, and Michigan, though some were still living in Ohio. By 1914, the titles were acquired. The First Presbyterian Church was given their title right away.

Eventually, the Board of Education received the title for the site of Timken Vocational High School.

Gladys Tannehill became the first woman to go up in a balloon when she accompanied pilot Leo Stevens in "Sky Pilot." They landed in Cairo in Stark County. Later she made a solo flight in "You and I," traveling over McDonaldsville. Her only complaint about her trip was that it was too short. She wanted "to go skimming through the clouds like lightning." Another early female balloonist was Blanche Vignos, vice president of the Ohio Federation of Women's Clubs. She went up with Leo Stevens in "The Ohio," landing north of Cuyahoga Falls. She thoroughly enjoyed her flight as well. "It was so calm and beautiful that my only emotion was of delight," she said.

For the 1909 Stark County Centennial celebration, double ascensions provided balloon races for spectators. "The Ohio" and "Sky Pilot" raced—"Sky Pilot" won. The following year was the last year of flying in Canton. With the advent of airplanes, people were less interested in unpredictable trips in a balloon. Frank S. wrote the club a letter in May 1910 from France urging them to think in terms of "heavier than air" flight instead.

But Canton's early days of flying would influence the future of aeronautics in this country through the lives of both Frank S. and Frank P. Lahm. When Wilbur Wright took his flying machine to France, Frank S. was one of his first passengers. Frank P. enjoyed a distinguished career as one of the few men in the army with air experience. He became a leading aeronaut and was a balloonist with the U.S. Signal Corps. On September 9, 1908 he flew with Orville Wright at Ft. Meyer Heights, Virginia for 6 minutes and 40 seconds. In July 1909 he was the passenger when Orville broke all records for an aeroplane carrying two men. They were in the air for one hour and 12 minutes, covering a distance of 50 miles at 40 miles per hour. President Taft was in the crowd.

In August 1909, Frank P. was chosen as one of two aviators to manipulate the Wright aeroplane, which the government had ordered for the army. He went on to become one of the first army pilots in the world, flying machines that were made of "spruce, piano wire, and faith." During World War I, Frank P. organized the American lighter-than-air service in France. He also coordinated the air arm of the Second Army, winning a Distinguished Service Medal. After the war, he was in charge of a huge training center at Duncan Field near San Antonio, Texas, which later became the Gulf Coast Air Corps Training Center. After retiring in 1941, he wrote the landmark book *How Our Army Grew Wings*, which became a standard classic in the field of aeronautics.

But this was not the only chapter in aeronautics history written in Canton. When William H. Martin invented his monoplane in Canton in 1909, it was the first of its type in the world. Most of the other early inventors—including the Wright brothers—were experimenting with a biplane design.

CANTON

Martin was born January 21, 1855 and graduated with the Class of 1872, where he had Anna McKinley as a teacher. Young Martin helped his father with the family rope making business, as they had done for generations since coming to America in 1745. Martin started "making things" at the age of 8. He invented a rope spinning machine that facilitated work for his father. He married Mary E. Pontius when he was 24, became a successful farmer, and had six children before his wife died in September 1893. He married Almina Holtz Pontius two years later and had three more children with her.

In his spare time, Martin studied engineering and surveying. He was incredibly detail-oriented and accurate. Plain Township hired him to draw a map for them, and he served as county surveyor from 1883 to 1885. Always one to keep his mind sharp, Martin joined a debating club at Brush College near Canton. At one of its meetings, he was asked to suggest a topic. When he chose "Resolved that man will fly," he was practically laughed out of the room! No one else would take the affirmative, so Martin debated alone against three other people. To everyone's surprise, he presented such a convincing argument he actually won the debate.

Shortly afterwards, Martin began to experiment with making toy planes that flew when propelled by rubber bands. He patented his toy flying machine on January 3, 1908. But he could not find a manufacturer who was interested in marketing and building his planes, so they were never produced.

The same year, Martin built his monoplane glider. It was a bold, new design with a single wing instead of an upper and lower wing. The balancing wings formed a V below the main wing. The plane was made of light wood and had an English broadcloth stretched over the wings, which his wife Almina sewed. The plane was towed by a horse or a Ford car in order to take flight. When he completed it in the winter of 1908–1909, he put runners on it instead of wheels so it could be tested on the snow.

To put his invention into context, Orville Wright had his first successful flight near Kitty Hawk on December 17, 1903. He went 120 feet in 12 seconds in a 27-mile-per hour wind. Wilbur Wright was able to travel 852 feet in 59 seconds later that day. These were hardly "flights" by today's standards, but they represented the first time humans left the confines of gravity by their own invention. It was a remarkable achievement. The Wrights patented their plane on May 22, 1906.

On January 12, 1909, Martin took his plane to the top of a hill. Old Billy, the family farm horse, was hitched to the front by a long rope. Martin sat in the plane and signaled for Old Billy to start running. He went up 25 feet in the air and traveled a distance of 200 feet before Old Billy got tuckered out and began to slow down. After the maiden flight, Almina piloted the plane several times, becoming the first woman in history to fly in a heavier-than-air machine. In fact, every member of the family enjoyed the plane, including the dog!

Martin had kept his plane a secret during the building phase, but he certainly couldn't hide the spectacle of his test flights. Soon he was the talk of the town, which helped him proceed with his plane. He wanted to demonstrate it in the East, but lack of funds prevented him from making the trip. William A. and L.A. Hoberdier financed his trip to New York that spring. In April 1909 he appeared before the New York Aeronautic Society, where he demonstrated his model plane powered by rubber bands. In May, Mr. and Mrs. Martin demonstrated the real thing at an air meet at Morris Park, New Jersey. His plane was one of the few that actually got into the air that day. In September, Martin let his granddaughter Blanch make solo flights, proving the safety of his design. He received Patent #935384 on September 28, 1909.

Early on, Martin wanted a motor for his plane so it would not have to rely on horses or automobiles to get airborne. He wrote to Frank S. Lahm in Paris inquiring about a motor. Frank S. wrote him back on March 3, 1909 and told him that any successful motor available was outrageously priced—it would have cost $10,000! Used motors could be found cheaper, but they were extremely unreliable. Frank S. advised Martin that a smaller motor would be coming out soon, and that he should wait until then.

At the end of 1909, lacking funds for further demonstrations and improvements, Martin dismantled his plane and stored in it in his garage. Seven years later, he was able to purchase a French Le Rhone rotary engine. Then a series of strange mishaps and tragedies prevented him from actually installing it. Thoburn T. Martin planned to install it but was killed in a sand slide in 1916 before he had a chance to finish the job. Again Martin waited. In 1927, Captain Charles Nungessor, a World War I French military ace aviator, agreed to install the motor. But he was killed in an attempt to make a trans-Atlantic flight. By this time, Martin had all but given up on motorizing his little plane. It had become a novelty anyway, and the expense did not seem practical.

In 1928, 16th District Congressman John McSweeny heard about the plane and came to Canton to study it. He reported his findings to the curators at the Smithsonian, who became interested in having the Martin plane for their collection. They asked Martin for it, and he had it crated and shipped to Washington, D.C. in January 1929. In 1936, the year before he died, Martin saw a man named Dennis R. Smith, who had visited the Smithsonian and saw the Martin plane displayed next to the *Spirit of St. Louis*. When he told Martin, who was then 81 years old, he said it was the happiest moment of his life. Martin was buried on Easter Sunday 1937, knowing that he had achieved national recognition for his contributions to the history of flight. In the 1980s, the McKinley Museum brought the plane back home to Canton on loan from the Smithsonian. Ownership was subsequently transferred to the McKinley Museum when the loan expired.

A select few were playing around with flight at the turn of the nineteenth century. Bicycles were all the rage for the rest of the population. The first high wheeled bicycle came to Canton in 1877, when Reginald H. Bulley came to Canton from England. His bicycle was the highest one around, standing at a height of 64 inches! The high wheeler had been introduced just a year earlier at the Centennial Exposition in Philadelphia.

By 1885, there were ten members of the Canton Bicycle Club. In October of that year, the club sponsored Bicycle Day at the County Fair, which was then held at Nimisilla Park. The horsemen didn't want the bicycles at the fair because they feared it would detract from their attention. They were certainly right about that! The bicycle races stole the show, attracting a crowd of 20,000 people. After that, the group decided their event was popular enough to stand on its own, and they dropped out of the county fair program.

The Stark County Bicycle Clubs jointly sponsored a state bicycle meet in September 1886. It was a three day affair, with one day each in Massillon, Canton, and Alliance. The safety bicycle had not yet been invented, so everyone was still riding the high wheelers. One hundred "wheelmen" came from across Ohio to participate in the state meet. After spending the first day in Massillon, the group pedaled over to Canton in the evening. The ride took a full hour. When they arrived, they stored their bicycles at Rink Vendom at Poplar (now Cleveland Avenue) and Third Street NW. At 8:00 they gathered at the Metropolitan Rink to watch bicycle tricks and a game of polo played on bicycles. At 10:30, the group sat down to a six course, $2 banquet at Landlord Barnett's Hotel, which lasted well into the night. At 7:00 the next morning, they took an 8-mile excursion before breakfast. Then they paraded to Meyers Lake, where they took a 15¢ steamboat ride to the Lake Park Hotel for a 60¢ waffle luncheon. That afternoon they biked out to Alliance for the third and final day of the meet.

Injuries from falling off the high wheelers were frequent, and though fatalities were rare, people were sometimes killed from a particularly bad fall. In 1888, the so called "safety bicycle" was introduced. It had two wheels of the same size and was considered a much safer ride. Before the invention of the safety bicycle, all of the riders of the high wheelers were men. It was not easy for a woman to ride a bicycle at that height while wearing a long skirt. Women began riding the safety bicycles when the center bar was dropped to accommodate their attire.

C.W. Keplinger was the first local to buy the new safety bicycle. Soon, everyone in Canton was riding a bicycle instead of taking a horse and buggy excursion. And the transition was fast. In 1892 there were 800 cyclists in Canton. In 1897 there were

4,000, and just three years later the number doubled to 8,000! There were 45 businesses involved in making or repairing bicycles in Canton, either as a primary or sideline venture. In 1896, John C. Dueber even joined the bicycle craze, constructing a special building adjoining the watch case factory for the production of bicycles. The Dueber Special bicycle sold for $85, and his bicycles were reported to be the favorite in town by 1899. In 1900 his watch case factory needed more space, so Dueber sold his bicycle stock to make room for the expansion.

People took bike excursions around the city and surrounding countryside. Members of the "Century Club" were admitted after riding 100 miles on a bike within a 24 hour time limit. Most stores, factories, and schools had bike racks for the convenience of shoppers, workers, and students.

Bicycle riding was just one of the many leisure activities available in Canton. In the 1910s, Nickelodeons were extremely popular. They showed one reel picture shows for just a nickel, which is how they got their name. It would only take a few years for multiple-reel films to be introduced, and admission went up to a dime. The theaters were equipped with a single projector; when one reel was finished, the operator put up a sign that read "One Moment Please" while the reels were switched.

A.H. Abrams is considered the "father of the Nickelodeon" in Canton. His 5¢ theater was located at 225 East Tuscarawas Street. His first ad appeared on September 2, 1906, with a synopsis of the two films he was showing: *The Wig Chase* and *Dream of the Rarebit Fiend*. These early films were silent and were often accompanied by live music played in the theater.

The multiple reel film was perfected in 1911, and other spots in town started to get into the movie business, including the Grand Opera House and the Auditorium. That year the Auditorium showed the $100,000 film *Dante's Inferno*. The Grand Opera House featured William A. Brady's *Baby Mine* and *The Bells of Justice*, a dramatization of Longfellow's "Bell of Atri." Other early films shown in Canton were *Death & Resurrection* (complete with pictures of the coronation of Pope Pius X), a western called *Tribal Law*, and *The Port of Doom*, the first marine detective drama.

Some of the early movie houses included the Orpheum, the Odeon, the Valentine, and the Alhambra, built in 1913 by Phil Bernower and Valentine L. Ney. The Alhambra celebrated its first Christmas by giving a present to each lady that came into the theater every afternoon except Saturday and Sunday. A special pitch urged the ladies to come in for a rest when they were tired of Christmas shopping.

In 1914, serials ran from week to week, leaving the lead characters on the brink of some horrible disaster, ensuring the viewer would come back to see how it all turned out. D.W. Griffith's landmark film *Birth of a Nation* was released on February 8, 1915, but Canton had to wait a year before seeing it. Ohio's governor banned it throughout the state for its "anti-Negro character," certainly a progressive opinion in a time where segregation and racism reigned supreme in most of the country.

On December 19, 1915, the Valentine showed pictures of the annual Army-Navy football game held at the Polo Grounds in New York City on November 27, almost a month after the game was played. The Valentine had been built the year before by Edward Bockius, who named it after his great grandfather, Valentine Bockius. Under Prohibition all of the movie theaters in town enjoyed a tremendous jump in attendance because the saloons were all forced to close down. The first "talkie" came to Canton in 1926 when *The Jazz Singer* opened at The Strand with Al Jolson singing "Mammy." The Palace and Loew's opened the same year.

The famed Auditorium opened in 1904 on Cleveland Avenue North between Fourth and Fifth Streets and was the fourth largest structure of its kind in the United States. It was dedicated on October 20, 1904 in front of a crowd of nearly 6,000. It was the most magnificent building Canton had ever seen. It had seating for 4,700 and boasted nearly 2 million square feet!

Advertisements for the new Auditorium listed numerous safety precautions in its construction. It was heated using steam with a plant outside the building located under the street. There was no cellar where combustible materials could be stored. There were 19 exits, and steel trusses were used in its construction. Upon completion, the building was turned over to the city, to be managed by the mayor and service director.

Organizers booked the best singers, musicians, orchestras, and speakers, including Sousa's Band, directed by the March King himself. Conventions, dances, and rallies were held in the City Auditorium as well. Famous evangelist Aimee Semple McPherson held a series of spectacular meetings in 1921, and Billy Sunday held his second big revival there, which continued for five weeks! The New York Philharmonic Orchestra played there, as did Enrico Caruso. The YMCA moved its lecture series to the Auditorium, and it was the site of McKinley High School graduation exercises.

The sporting events were unsurpassed, including championship boxing, wrestling matches, and basketball games—even roller polo on skates. Johnny Kilbane won the featherweight championship in 1912, and Jack Britton won the welterweight championship in 1919. McKinley High played its home basketball games there. The YMCA held amateur track meets at the Auditorium. There were also several charity events and benefits held in the early days. President Roosevelt and visiting dignitaries dined there when they were in town for the dedication of the McKinley National Memorial.

The space provided by the Auditorium made Canton a true convention city. Several organizations hosted events there, including the Ohio Sunday School Association,

United Spanish War Veterans of Ohio, Ohio Department of the GAR, the Ohio Grange, and the National Association of Letter Carriers. Famous speakers included Woodrow Wilson, William Jennings Bryan, and Carrie Nation.

Sadly, after just 36 years the City Auditorium fell into disrepair and was closed due to fire hazards. The deputy state inspector called the building "an ideal structure for a major catastrophe" because it was mostly made of wood. It was closed down in 1938. A major bond issue for $2.85 million worth of repairs failed to pass by a 2–1 margin in 1947. So after 12 years of debate on what to do with it, it was sold to the Cleveland Avenue Realty Company, which turned it into a parking garage.

In 1900 tennis and golf were gaining popularity nationwide, as were football and baseball. Canton had an amateur football team in 1903 and began hiring professional players the following year. The rivalry between the Canton Bulldogs and the Massillon Tigers that still exists today began in the early twentieth century with the professional teams. The high school teams adopted those names after the pro teams left for larger cities.

Pro football grew out of a pro baseball tradition that was already established in neighboring communities. Canton, Massillon, Barberton, and Akron played in baseball leagues that were constantly changing—Tri-State, Central, Buckeye, Ohio, and Middle Atlantic. Pro football actually began in Latrobe, Pennsylvania on August 31, 1895 when the first player was compensated for his talent. At the time, there were teams in upstate New York, New York City, Pittsburgh, and Philadelphia. Akron was the first city in the area to add a football franchise in 1903. Canton and Massillon soon followed, and football became a major pastime for both communities. Annual matches between the rival teams attracted large audiences and captured the attention of almost everyone in town.

Early football was a rough and tumble sport—19 players were killed playing the game in 1903. There was a great deal of confusion about the rules of the sport, and the brutality was incomparable. Rarely did a game go by without a broken collarbone or fractured leg. It got so bad that President Roosevelt called a meeting of college representatives at the White House in 1905 to reform and improve the game.

Canton's first team was called the Athletics. They were coached by William L. Day, son of William R. Day. He used home talent in combination with semi-pro or strictly amateur players. In 1904 the team started securing college players for weekend games, and Coach Day organized the Canton Athletic Club to help fund Canton's football, baseball, and basketball teams.

In 1906 the Athletics became the Bulldogs. The rivalry between Canton and Massillon was in full swing by then, with both communities supporting the teams financially and packing the stands for games. Even *The Repository* gave front page billing to the first Canton–Massillon game that year, when the Bulldogs beat the Tigers. But when the Bulldogs lost a second match, a Canton player was accused of throwing the game. He left town on the first train, and professional football was over in Canton for the next nine years.

With the scandal largely forgotten, Canton tried football again in 1915 when Ray McGregor and Ben Clark started another team. According to Stark County Historian E.T. Heald, the Canton–Massillon games in this new era were "hard fought and fairly played." Jim Thorpe came to town to play in two games with the Bulldogs in 1915. By this time, most of the home talent had been replaced by "imported" players from around the country. The venerable Thorpe led the Canton Bulldogs to their first World Championship in 1919. They repeated in 1922 and 1923. Then the team was bought out and moved to Cleveland.

In 1920 the Professional Football League was formed in Ralph Hay's Hupmobile dealership at Cleveland Avenue and Second Street SW. Hay owned the Canton Bulldogs. The objectives were to unify scattered teams, prevent contract jumping, and regulate the sport's rules and regulations. Each of the 12 teams were supposed to pay a $100 franchise fee, but it was waived because no team had that much money! At that time, most of the teams were located in mid-sized cities. They would soon leave for larger cities where they could draw larger crowds and make more money. Since Canton was the home of the first organized professional football league, it was an ideal location for the Pro Football Hall of Fame that would come to town 40 years later.

Canton got its second hospital in 1907 when Mrs. Rosa Klorer bought President McKinley's home on North Market after Ida's death on May 26 of that year. Sadly, preservation of a presidential home was not a priority at the time, so no effort was made to protect the home for future generations to enjoy.

Mrs. Klorer bought the home for $20,000 and turned it over to the Diocese of Cleveland as a memorial to her late husband, Herman Klorer. She and her brother Charles Lang requested that the Sisters of Charity of St. Augustine be put in charge of the hospital. Reverend Bishop Horstman agreed and came to Canton to establish Mercy Hospital.

The McKinley residence was converted into an 18-bed hospital. Mrs. McKinley's suite was transformed into a children's ward, which held a certain bittersweet irony since both the McKinleys' children had died young. The parlor where the President had heard of his 1896 presidential nomination via phone became the record room of the hospital. Community members helped furnish the chapel, private rooms, and departments, and sewing circles made linens. The hospital was opened and blessed on September 24, 1908, the Feast Day of Our Lady of Mercy. Two patients were admitted.

Like Aultman Hospital, Mercy soon found its needs were greater than the space of the original building. To make room for a new wing in 1928, the hospital removed the original McKinley home and deeded it to the Civitan Club of Canton. The group planned to move the house to Meyers Park and began raising funds to do so. It divided the house into four sections, and 30 men working 18 hours a day moved it. Before the group could raise enough money for restoration, the stock market crashed and the Civitan Club folded. The restoration plans were abandoned, and no one else in the community stepped forward to save the house. The Canton Fire Department removed the famous front porch after it started to sag. In 1934, the Canton Board of Health declared the house a nuisance, saying it was "in a filthy and unsanitary condition." In 1935, the Park Commission dismantled the home, recycling parts of the presidential residence to build park shelters. Parts of the house were saved by souvenir hunters, and some of the oak timbers went to the Canton Chamber of Commerce and the McKinley Lodge of Masons to make gavels. The iron gate from the house has been preserved at the McKinley Museum.

Mercy Hospital completed its new wing in 1930. The hospital built a nurse's home in 1942 and launched an expansion campaign to raise $1.5 million in 1948. A city the size of Canton at the time should have had 700 beds—between Aultman and Mercy there were only 492. Mercy needed to expand because of overcrowding. They were regularly postponing all non-essential surgeries for lack of space. They had no isolation room to control epidemics, and they were greatly overburdened in maternity.

The Timkens offered the H.H. Timken mansion and over 30 acres of land, appraised at over $202,000, as a gift to the hospital. When federal money was withdrawn, the Timken Foundation stepped in to help, and the hospital was renamed Timken Mercy Hospital in 1950. The Timken family was just as generous to Aultman Hospital with equal donations.

Though the tradition of the YMCA had been going strong in Canton for almost a century, Canton did not get a Young Women's Christian Association (YWCA) until 1909, 50 years after the YWCA was founded nationally. In the absence of their own group, women simply attended functions at the YMCA. In 1896 there were 125 members of the YMCA's Woman's Auxiliary. There was a special gym class just for women at $5 a quarter, and the Auxiliary sponsored a cooking school and a course in orchestral music. At Thanksgiving, the Auxiliary ran a soup kitchen for the needy.

In 1909, Anna Lowry Wheeler spoke to her Sunday school teacher, Mrs. Charles H. Poor, about organizing a YWCA in Canton. Within two weeks a meeting was held at the Methodist Church to investigate the feasibility of such a venture. By the end of the year, the women had obtained a charter for Canton's first Young Women's

Christian Association. Over the years membership grew from 1,000 in 1912 to 4,000 in 1949.

Committees formed to handle the functions of the new YWCA in the categories of membership, house, Bible study, educational, social, finance, gym, library, extension, and junior activities. Early on they organized a series of popular classes, including sewing, dress and shirtwaist making, cooking, millinery, English literature, French, German, mandolin, and guitar.

A main component of the YWCA was raising money for relief, especially during wartime. Some of the funds went towards scholarships so needy girls could go to camp. The Sunshine Society, a work group for girls aged 8–15, organized in 1911. In the early years, the girls learned to sew on bolts of gingham donated by Lew Zollars. They also learned to cook and do camp fire work. They collaborated with Traveler's Aid to meet late arriving trains. They also helped girls who were new in town find living quarters, which led to the creation of a city-wide register of suitable rooms for girls. The YWCA also held noonday meetings for working girls in several of Canton's plants and factories, including Gibbs, Republic Steel, Timken, and Troy Laundry.

Even as Canton focused on the moral improvement of its young women, a world crisis was looming on the horizon. Sparked by the assassination of Archduke Franz Ferdinand, heir to the throne of Austria-Hungary, by a Serbian nationalist secret society on June 28, 1914, war erupted around the world. A tangle of alliances drew several countries into the conflict. The United States finally entered the war in 1917, when Germany's policy of unrestricted submarine warfare threatened American commercial shipping interests.

Following the declaration of war, hundreds of Cantonians marched off to fight. As a symbol of their pride, soldiers' families displayed "service flags" in their windows. They were white flags with a red border and a blue star for each member of the household who had joined the war. When the blue star was replaced with a gold one, it meant that soldier was never coming home.

Even before officially entering the war, American industries worked hard to meet the demands of a wartime economy for the Allies. By this time, Canton's industries were leaders in their fields and had become powerhouses of production for the war effort. Diebold built all of the armor plating for tanks made in America. Berger Manufacturing Company constructed corrugated iron shelters for use in France. Union Metal Company built artillery ammunition chests, tools, and spare parts for the military. Hoover resurrected its leatherworks for the war effort.

An article in the August 19, 1917 issue of *The Repository* dramatized the contribution of Canton's industries to the war by humanizing the experience of a soldier:

When the soldier puts on his leggings in the morning he will be using some of the local manufacturer's products. When he looks at his wrist he probably will see leather straps made here. When the mess call is given he will pick up enamelware dishes made here and hurry to get some of the food taken out of tin cans manufactured in Canton. He may be driving an automobile truck whose engine has been manufactured in this city or he may be helping to "feed" shells into one-pound guns, whose metallic parts were rolled and made in different mills in Canton. Whenever a soldier is called to report to the Captain for delinquency he probably will watch the Captain take a small roll call book from a metal desk which had its origin in local plants. When the soldiers are fighting in the first line trenches they may be commanded to advance and the command may be given to put on their gas masks. These are also being manufactured in large quantities here. Parts for large guns, saddles, harness and many of the other important fittings of the army are also to be manufactured in this city. Some of the orders booked here, it is said, will take many months to complete.

That same day the newspaper reported that Gilliam Manufacturing Company had received a government contract to make 90,000 gas masks—that is, 3,000 a day.

Canton's citizens were proud supporters of the war on the homefront, raising over $20 million in five Liberty Loan campaigns. Bond rallies were held in the City Auditorium, at Public Square, and in the factories. Children bought Thrift Stamps in school for as little as a few cents each, which they could collect in a booklet until they had enough to buy a war bond. Food was not rationed during World War I, but some things were scarce. Patriotic citizens followed their own schedule of "meatless" and "wheatless" days to conserve.

In September 1918, Canton was one of the first communities to answer Ohio Governor Cox's request that "Taps" be played across the state every evening at 5:30. Professor W.E. Strassner played "Taps" that first Friday night, dressed in a Canton Guards uniform, from the tower of the courthouse. *The Repository* reported that the mournful song was being played to "send the thought across the housetops that Canton's soldiers in France had completed their day's work. As the first clear notes of the bugle sounded, thousands of heads were bowed in prayer and thousands of men and women stood at attention."

Many of Canton's citizens were of German descent and had German names. Since Germany was the enemy in World War I, the German-American community became sensitive about its heritage. German newspapers stopped publication. New Berlin changed its name to North Canton. And sauerkraut became "Liberty Cabbage."

To help disseminate information, Jack Barnes organized the Canton Four Minute Men who presented talks, theater pieces, and motion pictures explaining the causes of the war and what was going on at the front. The Canton Adcraft Club, a service organization, launched ad campaigns for war savings. Stark County became the first county with a population over 100,000 to go over quota in pledges and cash sales, winning state and national recognition. Savings stamps sales reached $3.4 million. When Governor Cox visited Canton, 25,000 people participated in a parade that ended at the McKinley National Memorial. It was the largest parade in Ohio.

The Canton Chapter of the American Red Cross was founded in February 1917. The Allies called on the Red Cross for supplies and relief work. Canton was ready. Women knitted scarves, sleeveless sweaters, and socks for the soldiers. In February 1918, a Junior Red Cross Chapter formed in Canton.

In September 1918—in the midst of war—a flu epidemic hit Canton. City government ordered several public places to close, including movie theaters, churches, saloons, pool rooms, club rooms, and public halls. Schools closed their doors for seven weeks. People were prohibited from congregating or loitering on the street or in other public places. Stores were ordered to close early on Saturdays to cut down on foot traffic through businesses. Advertising of special sales was to be "discontinued at once." New street car regulations went into effect immediately. All ventilators were required to be open, only seating capacity was allowed, and at least two windows had to be open on each car. In public, people wore masks to protect themselves.

Fred F. "Sticks" Sanderson, a telegrapher at *The Repository*, was the first to receive the news over the wire that the armistice had been signed at 2:45 a.m. on November 11, 1918. As reported in *The Repository*, a few of Canton's citizens who had waited up all night "in hopes that the armistice would be signed immediately started a celebration in the business district." At 3:30 a.m., the fire bell rang out and the factory whistles blew. People shared the good news with sleepy neighbors who opened their windows to see what all the fuss was about. An impromptu crowd assembled at Public Square, ignoring the flu epidemic ban on congregating. Mayor Charles Poorman announced a grand parade would be held the following afternoon, and he invited all factory workers, bands, patriotic organizations, and civic groups to join in. By 8:00 a.m. there was complete chaos on the Square, as people celebrated victory overseas. Thayer's Military Band led the parade, playing "Over There." *The Repository* had this to say about the festivities the morning after:

> With all ordinary affairs of business almost at a standstill, Canton Monday
> afternoon joined hands with the rest of the nation and celebrated the dawn

> of peace by staging one of the biggest and most sincere demonstrations of its history. . . . Working men from practically every shop and factory in the city who during the past months had labored faithfully night and day to produce the materials so essential to victory armed themselves with noise-making devices, climbed onto trucks and took part in the parade…From the Thayer Military band which was in the lead to the last decorated auto, the parade was replete with special stunts, patriotic floats and illuminating suggestions relative to the disposal of the Kaiser.

Cars and trucks decorated with flags pulled the guest of honor—Kaiser Wilhelm, who was hung in effigy—down the dusty streets. The merriment continued into the wee hours of the morning.

Even though Canton was celebrating, the flu epidemic was still on. It wasn't until December 1, 1918 that the city government lifted the ban on church services. Schools reopened the next day, but any student showing even the slightest sign of sickness was sent home. In Canton, there were a total of 10,000 cases of flu, which often developed into deadly pneumonia. When it was all said and done, 463 people were dead, a number far greater than war casualties. There were 119 soldiers from Stark County killed in the war. Only 63 were from Canton.

The following year on the Fourth of July, more grand patriotic festivities took place. A highlight of the day was the burial of "It Can't Be Done." It was said that "Can't" was killed by the Liberty Loan Organization, murdered by a city that out sold its quota in war bonds. A mock funeral service was held in Public Square. Attorney George H. Clark delivered the eulogy, saying:

> We are met to pay our last tribute to the local member of the great family of It Can't Be Done. The departed was of ancient and historic lineage. The family has existed and flourished in our midst since the settlement of this city, and it came to the fullness of its career in April 1917.
>
> With the declaration of war, It Can't Be Done saw the opportunity to justify for all time the existence of the doctrine of failure. We had to raise an army. It Can't Be Done snarled at our heels. We had to raise money for national defense. It Can't Be Done yelped discord and growled failure.
>
> But, the people grew in thought, in spirit, in resolve, in spirituality. They wearied not of well doing. They joined shoulder to shoulder in mighty effort. They kicked out of the way the snappers and the yelpers. They chastised the big growlers and they interred the vicious and the malicious.

> And so undeterred, unafraid and determined, they marched forward to
> glorious victory, and starved to death for lack of friends It Can't Be Done
> in this community. It died, and we are met to bury it deep for all time.
> Peace to its ashes.

A 4-foot square bronze plaque was lowered onto the sidewalk at the southeast corner of the Stark County Courthouse. At the top it read, "Here Lies It Can't Be Done." The message ended with the phrase, "May He Long Be Dead." Over the years, many local residents brought their children downtown to teach them a lesson in perseverance. The plaque was later moved from its downtown location to its current home outside the McKinley Museum.

The funeral kicked off a series of activities commemorating our victory in World War I and the soldiers who fought and died. A plane and a blimp flew over the crowd, and medals were presented to the military.

When the 308th Engineers Veteran Association was organized August 21, 1918, three of the top six officers were Canton natives. Jay L. Goodin was president, Wilbur C. Hushour was first vice president, and Ernest Duerr was second vice president. On that summer day in 1968, the veterans celebrated the 50th anniversary of their unit's first engagement in France—the Aisne-Marne offensive, which was fought from July 26 to August 6, 1918—at the Hotel Onesto. In July 1968, 30 of the original 150 Stark County veterans who had joined 308th Engineers were still living.

Chapter Six

THE ROARING TWENTIES AND THE GREAT DEPRESSION

The Roaring Twenties were a time of great celebration and prosperity for the entire nation. The war was over, the stock market was soaring, and life could finally get back to normal. Hemlines went up, hair was cut short, and the Charleston was all the rage. So much had changed, both nationally and locally. In 1860, 21 percent of the population of Stark County lived in the three largest towns—Canton, Massillon, and Alliance. By 1920, 71 percent lived in the cities. Most homes now had electricity, and most kitchens had a gas stove for cooking. Canton's industries were booming, not only from the successful war effort, but because of smart business decisions and superior marketing to consumers beyond northeast Ohio.

By World War I, Timken bearings were used in 90 percent of trucks and buses in the world. In 1918, tests proved that Timken bearings would increase the life of Ford front wheels three to five times. The following year, Ford signed a contract with Timken for the mass production of his Model T. With an annual production of 6 million cars, Timken produced 210 million individual anti-friction bearings for parts like wheels, pinions, differentials, and steering gears.

But early on, the company saw the need to diversify so not all of its production was tied up in the automobile industry. They began to experiment with new applications for their roller bearings in things like mine cars and machine tools. As a result, Timken bearings were used in every kind of machinery where friction is a problem, including equipment for steel mills, oil fields, aircraft, and farming. Timken bearings could be found in paper mill machines of the Great Lakes Paper Company, Ltd., the newspaper press of the *Chicago Tribune*, and in US Navy equipment.

Research continued during the Depression to discover new uses for Timken bearings. They developed a rock bit for mining, which became standard equipment in 75 percent of mines by 1939. But what Timken really wanted was a contract with the locomotive industry. Timken began supplying roller bearings to two locomotives on the New York Central line in 1928. The following year they had equipped 33 more. In 1930 Timken ordered a steam locomotive and christened it *Timken 1111*—known as "The Four Aces." It was the first steam locomotive completely equipped with Timken roller bearings. Timken launched a major sales pitch by loaning The Four Aces to 14 different railroads in 18 months. The train covered 100,000 miles in test runs, proving the durability of Timken bearings in the railroad industry. Timken then sold The Four Aces to the Northern Pacific Railroad, where it covered 1.6 million miles by 1955.

The incredibly successful demonstration of The Four Aces earned Timken orders from three railroads. They were positioned to launch a massive campaign to increase railroad sales, but by then the Great Depression had taken a toll on all industries, including the railroad.

Hoover also enjoyed great success during World War I and into the 1920s and beyond. In 1917, the White House purchased Hoovers. In 1919 King George V of England stopped at the Hoover booth at the Ideal Home Exhibit in London and requested one for the palace. Queen Marie of Romania bought one in 1927, as did the Prince of Wales in 1933. When the *Queen Mary* made her maiden voyage to the United States in 1936, she had 42 Hoovers aboard.

Products manufactured in Canton found their way into some pretty high profile projects. Several parts used in the construction of the Holland Tunnel in New York City were made in Canton. So was the hub of the propeller on Charles Lindbergh's *Spirit of St. Louis*. Canton also boasted the largest brick paving company in the world.

A highlight of the 1920s was the opening of the new Stern & Mann department store in 1925. Built by Melbourne Construction Company of Canton, the colossal new building on the corner of Cleveland Avenue and Tuscarawas Street was a gorgeous structure built with the finest materials. Italian marble, walnut, rosewood, and mirrors created an elegant shopping experience that was unparalleled in Canton. The wide, spacious aisles were complimented by two elegant elevators with elaborately detailed bronze grillwork.

On opening day, customers raved about it in the pages of *The Repository*. "It's a beautiful store—one of the most beautiful I've ever seen." "Those walls of walnut panels and mirrors made me feel as if I were in a spacious drawing room." "What impressed me was the convenience of everything. There wasn't a thing missing to add to the comfort of the woman who goes there to shop." "Did you ever see so beautiful an elevator front?"

Around 1910, women began buying ready-to-wear clothes instead of fabric to make dresses themselves. This allowed Stern & Mann to expand their merchandise dramatically by offering the latest fashions for women to buy off the rack. The new store provided plenty of space to stock multiple sizes of the same outfit, as well as a wide variety of accessories. The new shoe department offered customers furniture that resembled a "little parlor" as they tried on the latest in footwear. The modern storage system boasted "shelves for the shoes . . . built so that each box will have its own compartment, and there will be no boxes stacked one upon the other." A sleek system of tiny drawers in the glove department made it possible for the gloves to be "brought forth at Madame Shopper's request" with elegance and ease. The little drawers in the hosiery department had glass faces so the merchandise could be seen without being handled. Special rooms in the millinery department allowed shoppers to view the more exclusive models of hats in privacy and luxury. Lingerie from France, silk from the Orient, and the newest gowns from Paris made Stern & Mann the place to shop.

Meyers Lake was booming as well. During the World War I years, there were new vaudeville acts every week, Madame Eckert the fortune teller, a Japanese tea garden, and plenty of free attractions like tight rope walkers, bicycle riders on a high wire, and a man shot out of a cannon.

The Lake View Hotel was owned and operated by George Sinclair and his son Carl. The family continued to acquire rides and concessions throughout the 1910s and 1920s. By 1924 they owned several and were in the middle of constructing the grand Moonlight Ballroom. The advent of the automobile was really hurting Northern Ohio Traction & Light Company. People were starting to travel independently in their own cars, so it became less feasible for rail companies to own and promote parks like Meyers Lake. They wanted to get out of the amusement park business, so George Sinclair took over management of the park.

After the 1926 season ended, the Sinclairs rebuilt the entire park. They demolished many of the old buildings and rides and put up new ones. They spent $250,000 in the first year, adding things like Bluebeard's Castle near the entrance and several new rides, including the Tilt-a-Whirl, Dodg-em, and a new ferris wheel. They also opened a zoo, with lions, tigers, hyenas, mountain lions, rhesus monkeys, leopards, buffalo, birds, and prairie dogs. They intended to make the zoo one of the largest in Ohio, but the expense forced them to abandon the idea after just eight years. The "new" Meyers Lake opened on May 21, 1927.

Fire revisited the park several times, leveling landmarks. In 1929 the Lake View Hotel burned to the ground. In 1936 the old roller rink burned. In 1939 the new roller rink, the zoo barn, and the old carousel were all destroyed by fire.

The Sinclairs brought a new merry-go-round to Meyers Lake in 1939. It was hand carved in 1914 by Stein and Gold Stein of New York. Each horse was an exquisite piece of artwork, with glass eyes and lots of roses draped over their bodies. There were a total of 48 stallions on brass poles with two chariots, a Wurlitzer organ, and two bellows—one for music and one for the drums and cymbals. The Sinclairs loved flowers and planted thousands of petunias on the grounds of Meyers Lake. There were so many, the flower is still associated with the park.

CANTON

In the 1930s, Laffing Sal (later known as Beulah the Laffing Lady) came to the park and stood at the entrance of the Laff-in-the-Dark ride. Many residents of Canton recall with fond memories the days when they courted their future spouses and stole a kiss or two on that ride. Laffing Sal cackled non stop. Reportedly the manufacturer took a retired opera singer out on the town, got her drunk, and told her "off-color" jokes until she was in hysterics. They secretly recorded her laughter and used it to animate Laffing Sal.

The Sinclairs built the Moonlight Ballroom as an open air dance hall in 1924. It was originally called the Moonlight Gardens and was the largest open air dance pavilion in Ohio. It was 36,000 square feet, with an orchestra stand in the center of the floor. A roof was added in 1926 or 1927. It was the hottest night spot in Canton for many years. Some of the era's greatest stars performed there, including Cab Calloway, Sammy Kay, Benny Goodman, Perry Como, Ella Fitzgerald, Glenn Miller, and Tommy Dorsey. In 1942, a second Moonlight Gardens was built adjacent to the Moonlight Ballroom. Summer dances were held outside, and the Ballroom was used the rest of the year. Many area proms were held at Meyers Lake over the years.

With the rise of super-sized amusement parks like Cedar Point, attendance started to drop off at Meyers Lake in the 1960s. The Sinclairs decided to call it quits after almost half a century of running the park. The Canton landmark closed its gates for the last time after the 1972 season.

A Massillon realtor bought the Moonlight Ballroom for $300,000 in 1977. After extensive remodeling, it opened the following year. The largest crowd since the reopening came to see the Glenn Miller Orchestra under the direction of Jimmy Henderson on January 6, 1979. That night, a massive fire completely destroyed the Moonlight Ballroom. To date, no one else has tried to bring back the magical summer days of Meyers Lake. The abandoned rides and concessions have long since been torn down, and no sign of the popular amusement park exists today.

No picture of the 1920s is complete without acknowledging the rapid rise of the automobile. In a few short years, Henry Ford's Model T had revolutionized life in America. Reliable personal transportation at a reasonable cost brought the freedom of travel to the masses. Canton was typical of many communities across the country. In the 1910s, there were no traffic lights, no parking lots, no gas tax, no one-way streets, and few paved roads outside the city. The speed limit was 10 miles per hour in the business district of the city and 20 miles per hour everywhere else.

The Canton Automobile Club was founded in 1910 by J.H. Kenny and W.A. Hoberdier. Beginning as a social group, the two men gathered up a group of pioneer motorists at the Elks Club. With membership dwindling, the group was reorganized in 1917 and had over 4,000 members by 1925. The Auto Club became a political activist organization, lobbying to secure paved roads throughout the county. When most of the roads were not paved, the Auto Club was considered the source of information about passable roads and detours. They were also an important part of the safety movement, supplying the city with stop signs, parking signs, and red signal lanterns for dangerous areas. In 1922 they instituted a revolutionary free towing service for members up to 10 miles outside of Canton.

In 1920, Canton city council passed the first parking ordinance requiring cars to parallel park on downtown streets. It was passed despite strong opposition from both the Auto Club and the merchants who wanted angle parking instead. Canton got its first traffic light in 1923 at the corner of Market Avenue and Tuscarawas Street, in the heart of downtown. It was a semaphore turned by hand. Lights soon followed at other prominent intersections. Second Street NW became Canton's first one-way street between Market and McKinley in 1923. Paul E. Meyers opened Canton's first parking lot at the corner of Cleveland Avenue and Fourth Street NW, but nobody parked their cars there so the lot was closed.

In 1928, the Canton police blotter began to break arrests and accidents into categories. Car related incidents included:

2,637 traffic accidents

22 traffic deaths

608 traffic injuries

6,988 traffic tickets

573 traffic arrests (453 for reckless driving)

611 stolen cars

119 DWIs

87 car thieves arrested

Traffic problems listed in the report included congestion; lack of adequate traffic police; reckless, careless, and inexperienced drivers; speeding; and jaywalking.

Traffic violations were not the only problem Canton had in the 1920s. Prohibition had given rise to a growing national crisis—The Mafia. Making alcohol illegal created an opportunity for crime rings to smuggle the forbidden beverage, with an incredible tax-free profit. "Speakeasies" sprang up all over the country. The unsuccessful 18th Amendment was eventually repealed with the 21st in 1933, but the damage had already been done. Crime families had amassed fortunes that allowed them access to political machines and often control of entire towns. Canton, now a city of 100,000, became known as "Little Chicago" for its reputation as a haven for organized crime.

CANTON

The *Canton Daily News*, a publication known for its progressivism and civic reform, was hard at work exposing the underworld. The city was shocked when publisher Don R. Mellett was gunned down in July 1926. How could something so awful happen in Canton? The complex story that unfolded in the days following the murder was full of twists and turns, and it was truly stranger than fiction.

Don Mellett came from the *Times-Press* in Akron where he had been an advertising salesman. He was hired as business manager of the *Daily News* in January 1925 and was promoted to publisher within a year. He was staunchly opposed to alcohol. Walter Vail, a close friend of Mellett's who was with him the night he died, remembers how his crusade in Canton began. "One evening we were in a Canton restaurant when two young teenage couples walked in," Vail said. "Despite Prohibition, they were obviously drunk. One of the girls turned sick and rushed outside. Don watched them with disgust. He vowed to me that the next day he would begin investigating where the booze was coming from in this town."

Mellett kept his word. He ran story after story with banner headlines screaming corruption as high up as the chief of police. Crime reports became a priority at the *Daily News*, making the front page most of the time. Between October 1925 and July 1926, the *Daily News* wrote 243 major editorials on Canton affairs. *The Repository* ran 83 during the same time period.

Some charged Mellett was exaggerating the crime in Canton. They thought he was making their city look bad with his constant barrage of crime stories. Others went as far as to accuse him of making up crime to sell more newspapers. The truth was, illicit liquor was easy to obtain, and those who controlled the flow were becoming rich. Other than that, there wasn't much crime in Canton. The underworld and law enforcement jointly made sure of that. The only bootleggers who ever got arrested were outsiders trying to work themselves into someone else's territory. Still, gambling and prostitution were on the rise, and the political machine wasn't going to do anything about it. Mellett wanted to help rid Canton of these social ills.

His crusade began with the following editorial on New Year's Day 1926:

> It is the opinion of the Daily News that Canton needs cleaning up. Bootlegging, gambling and houses of prostitution are running wide open in flagrant violation of the law. If Chief Lengel denies this, proof is available to him. . . . As Chief of Police, Mr. Lengel is the key to the situation of cleaning up Canton. If he can't do the job, no matter how good his intentions, he should resign or be removed. Thus, Mr. Lengel, we extend our New Year's greetings: Get busy, or get out.

The Roaring Twenties and the Great Depression

Early in 1926, Mayor Sanford A. Swarts, who had been backed by the *Daily News* in the election the year before, finally fired Lengel on the grounds that he was negligent in performing his duties. Lengel was eventually reinstated, after a Civil Service Commission chaired by Price Janson voted 2 to 1 to hire him back. Lengel sued the *Daily News* for $50,000 for defamation of character. Mellett targeted Janson next, charging that he was just as corrupt as Lengel. In July 1926, Janson was removed from his position.

In June, Mellett had started getting anonymous threats. His brother Lloyd insisted Don get a bodyguard. He hired George Beresford, one of Mellett's sources inside the police department. He only stood guard for a few weeks before the brothers decided they were overreacting. But on July 11, Mellett answered the phone and heard a voice say something bad was planned for him. He went out and bought a gun and sat out on his porch all night.

Four days later on July 15, 1926, the Vails and Melletts went to the Molly Stark Club dance at Bast Hall on Market Avenue. Mellett had been one of the founders of the club, whose purpose was to welcome new couples to town. They stopped at Bamberger's Restaurant on West Tuscarawas Street before returning to the Mellett home at the corner of West Tuscarawas Street and Claremont Avenue around 11:30 p.m. The two couples sat on the front porch talking. At 12:30 a.m. they went inside to have some coffee in the kitchen. Mellett went out to the garage to put his car away. They heard the garage door open, then they heard shots.

"Bullets splintered the back windows of the house," said Vail. "One came through the kitchen window and missed my head by a quarter inch. I felt its hot breeze as it went by." Vail got up and ran outside and found Mellett slumped over, with a gunshot wound to his head. It took the police 22 minutes to respond.

Suddenly, Canton realized there must be something to Mellett's allegations in the *Daily News*. He had uncovered something that was bad enough to get him killed. Who could argue the truth of his claims, now that he had been gunned down?

Most people believed the Canton Police Department could not be trusted with the investigation. Ora Slater, a private investigator from Cincinnati, was hired using a reward fund that was started by H.H. Timken, former owner of the *Daily News*. In an article that appeared the Friday of the murder, Timken said:

> Like most citizens, I thought Mellett was exaggerating this (crime) condition and paid little attention to it. This horrible murder has forced me to think back and now I recognize that Mellett was right. This murder is a revenge murder—a warning to the citizens of Canton that anyone daring

to question the right and power of the underworld to operate as they see fit
is in danger of his life.

Timken gave the first $5,000 to the fund, and by that evening the total reached
$11,000. When all was said and done, the fund swelled to $25,275.

Slater arrived in Canton on July 17 and had the whole crime solved in four days. A
man named William Betzler came to see the detective in his hotel room. He reported
seeing an acquaintance in town a few weeks before the murder who he had not seen
in seven years. The friend told him he was in Canton to "do a job." He said he was
"playing for high stakes" and was "hooked up with the high muckety-mucks" in town.
Thursday night he showed Betzler a revolver and refused a drink, saying the "job was
on" for that night.

This friend was Patrick E. McDermott, who was the son of a wealthy mining family
from Nanty Glo, Pennsylvania. Betzler told Slater he came to him rather than going
to the police with his information because McDermott had bragged that someone in
the police department was in on it.

A few days later, another piece of the puzzle waltzed into Slater's hotel room. Steve
Kascholk told the detective he met McDermott on a streetcar in Cleveland and asked
him for a job. McDermott told him he was going to Massillon, where a friend named
Ben Rudner had a job for him. Rudner had been convicted of robbery in 1915 and
was arrested again in 1921 for liquor law violations. A man named Paul Kitzig was
arrested with Rudner on the liquor charge and had turned state's evidence against
Rudner. On August 10, 1921, Kitzig was shot to death in a field north of Meyers Lake.
His murder was unsolved.

Mellett had told Vail a few days before he was shot that he had uncovered who had
killed Kitzig. "Don told me he was going to publish the name," Vail said. "I believe
that with that, Don signed his own death warrant. They killed him before that name
reached print."

Rudner, McDermott, and Kascholk met with gangster Louis Mazer, who took
them to Canton and showed them Mellett's house. They talked about "beating up an
editor," but Kascholk sensed they were talking about something worse than that. He
got nervous and went back to Cleveland.

Slater had put all the pieces of the murder plot together. Now all he needed to do
was track down the participants and arrest them. Mazer was arrested on a separate
liquor charge in August and was already in custody when murder indictments were
handed down to Mazer, Rudner, and McDermott in September. Detective Floyd
Streitenberger, a police officer who would later be incriminated as a conspirator, was

at a marksmanship competition in Buffalo. He rushed back to Canton to give Mazer an alibi, saying they were together at Streitenberger's house talking about a sick police dog.

McDermott's brother set him up by claiming that their mother was sick in Nanty Glo. When he showed up at home, the brother turned him over to Slater.

McDermott's trial began December 8, 1926. His only defense was that Kascholk had been in on the plot and backed out. His lawyer tried to argue that Mellett had made many enemies in Canton, any of whom might have tried to kill him. *Daily News* writer Dennis R. Smith reported that McDermott himself damaged his own case:

> His face was almost crimson. His beady eyes darted evasively everywhere about the courtroom. He told his story on direct examination with a monotony that was maddening and his voice conveyed a bored whine that never changed its inflection. He refused to answer some of the questions. Others he answered in such a way that it was evident to all that heard him that he was lying.

The state had 52 witnesses, but none could place McDermott at the scene. Still, the jury convicted him—on Christmas Eve—and he was sentenced to life in prison.

Rudner's trial began on February 7, 1927. Despite a substantial alibi, he was convicted of second degree murder and sentenced to life.

During Mazer's trial, it came out that he and Streitenberger had met on the night of the murder at the home of Doll Carey, owner of one of Canton's many prostitution houses. It was doubtful the two men were talking about sick police dogs. The testimony led to the indictment of Streitenberger on March 3, 1927. Mazer had turned state's evidence against Streitenberger in hopes of getting a reduced sentence. Mazer told the court that at about 12:30 a.m. he and Streitenberger were driving around Mellett's neighborhood where McDermott was waiting for an opportunity to shoot him. After hearing sirens, they went to the fairgrounds where they had planned to meet up with McDermott. He told them "the angels were talking to him now."

Streitenberger's defense remained that he was at his own house talking to Mazer about a sick dog. He was convicted on May 20, 1927 and got life.

Streitenberger and Mazer then joined forces to testify against Lengel, who was also indicted for murder on June 8, 1927. Two days later Mazer plead guilty to manslaughter. Lengel was convicted on July 17, 1927 but got a new trial on a technicality. Streitenberger suddenly refused to testify, and there was no case without him. So Lengel was acquitted. He died a bitter man fighting for his police pension.

Rudner was eventually released after several parole attempts. Streitenberger died in prison. Mazer served his sentence for manslaughter and was released. As part of his sentence, McDermott was placed in solitary confinement every year on July 16. He escaped several times, making the FBI's Top Ten Most Wanted List. After being captured for the last time, he agreed to be infected with tuberculosis in an experiment to find a cure. He died in 1971 in Lima State Hospital.

Despite all of the investigations, a murder weapon was never found. Some believed that Streitenberger, not McDermott, was the real killer. They believed McDermott was too drunk or too high to shoot straight, and that his bullets were the ones that went wild, almost killing Vail in Mellet's kitchen. Streitenberger was an expert police marksman. In one of the trials, a neighbor testified that he saw two men running from the scene. Another claimed to have seen a car with Pennsylvania plates hanging around the neighborhood.

Price Janson remained adamant for decades that Mellett had exaggerated Canton's crime scene. In an interview when he was 80 years old, Janson acknowledged there was prostitution, bootlegging, and drug traffic, but said there was no more crime in Canton than in any other urban area during Prohibition. Years after the Mellett murder, it came out that a Cherry Avenue hotel called the New Barnett had been a temporary hideout for such notorious crime bosses as Pretty Boy Floyd and Machine Gun Kelley. Another sensational murder happened in 1953 when John Nickles was shot to death. He was a partner in a bootlegging joint in the 1930s and was involved in illegal gambling in the 1940s and 1950s. He was beaten in the face and shot with a .38 caliber revolver. His murder was never solved.

Coverage of the Mellett murder made the front page in almost every major newspaper in the country, including *The New York Times*, *Washington Post*, and the *St. Louis Dispatch*. *The New York Times* ran the story on the front page for five days straight, and the index lists 71 stories about Mellett from July 17, 1926 to March 27, 1928.

The *Daily News* won a Pulitzer Prize for its coverage of the crime scene in Canton in 1926. The paper built a new building, laying the cornerstone one year after Mellett's murder. The building was finished in 1928. Sadly, the Depression forced the *Daily News* out of business, and it was bought by Brush-Moore Newspapers in 1930, owners of *The Repository*.

By far the *Daily News* was not the only victim of a faltering economy in the 1930s. When the stock market crashed on October 24, 1929, this country was plummeted into the worst economic disaster in history. Despite a soaring stock market, the economy was actually very unstable in the 1920s. The distribution of wealth was incredibly uneven. The boom was based on borrowed money and false optimism, and like a deck of cards, it crumbled before everyone's eyes.

The Roaring Twenties and the Great Depression

During the Depression, times were as tough in Canton as they were everyplace else in the country. People had to make due with less, and companies had to find ways to stay afloat in an unhealthy economy. Anxiety and depression were commonplace. People were literally starving. Children would have long-term effects from lack of proper nutrition. Multiple families were crowded into houses. Everyone was struggling.

Hoover began to make die castings commercially for other manufacturers who could not handle their own production. This helped Hoover to utilize factory space and provide employment for local workers. Smart business decisions allowed Hoover to fare better than many companies during the Depression. They experienced fewer layoffs than most businesses of comparable size.

In 1931 Hoover inaugurated a suggestion plan to encourage employees to submit ideas on improvements for the business. Management gave cash awards of up to $1,000 for the best ideas. Thousands of suggestions earned employees thousands of dollars.

Despite high unemployment and abject poverty, Canton experienced a cultural renaissance in the 1930s. People may have had less money, but they did have more leisure time. This rebirth helped create the Canton Art Institute (now the Canton Museum of Art), the Players' Guild, the Canton Symphony, and the Canton Civic Opera.

In 1936 the Canton Art Institute grew out of a little Civic Art Gallery established two years earlier. In addition to displaying fine art, the Art Institute conducted art classes at the Canton Public Library. Then, in 1939 a secret benefactor made it possible for the institute to make the Frank E. Case Mansion its new permanent home. Upon his death, it was made public that Fred A. Preyer was the anonymous donor. In February 1941, Henry Milligan's art treasures were donated to the institute.

The Player's Guild was organized in 1932 by Mr. and Mrs. Bernard Truxton. Without a theater of their own, plays were performed in the Jewish Center and in the old Masonic Temple until 1937. For the next few years, the Player's Guild floated around, giving performances at whatever venue was available to them. Then in 1940, the Case Mansion Coach House was turned over to them.

The Canton Symphony Orchestra was formed on January 26, 1938. It was sponsored by the Junior Chamber of Commerce. Richard W. Oppenheim was the first director. They held their first concert on February 16, 1938 at the Auditorium, which became their concert hall until the building was condemned in 1940. After that, the orchestra played in various high school auditoriums.

The Canton Civic Opera was started in 1939. Boris Goldovsky was the first director, and Mrs. Basil Thurin was the first president. Their first opera, *Bartered Bride*, was held at the Timken Vocational Auditorium on January 19 and 20, 1940.

CANTON

Surviving the Depression required creativity and new ways of thinking. At age 32, Dallas L. Hostetler was the youngest Chamber of Commerce manager of a city of over 100,000. He was responsible for outlining the plans and guiding Canton's innovative approach to community problems during the hardest economic times the city—and the nation—had ever seen.

In the bleak and daunting years of the Depression, Canton was heralded as a fine example of what could be accomplished by working together as a community. Hostetler held a series of intentionally small "town meetings" to address community problems. Citizens voiced their suggestions, complaints, and thoughts about issues directly related to their neighborhoods. People became invested in solving problems because they were allowed to be direct participants in the solutions. An individual who suggested an idea became its champion and worked diligently to see it through and make it happen. As a result, in 1935 there were four times as many active workers on community projects in Canton than there were the year before.

Four main themes were raised in these town meetings. First, people recognized the need to keep the industries Canton had, while seeking out new industries and encouraging them to come to town. The Canton Development Corporation grew out of this idea and was organized to assist plants with expansion plans. They raised $25,000 to support their projects.

Second, citizens asked, "What can be done to make Canton a place where industry wants to come?" They decided that first and foremost, people want happiness and a place to play. So Canton launched a $500,000 park and playground program to create spaces families could use for recreation. They planned an open space park for every section of town, including a 40-acre arboretum, swimming pools, horseshoe and tennis courts, comfort stations, baseball diamonds, rustic walking paths, bridges, and a municipal stadium. They received donations of money, land, and materials to turn these projects into reality.

The third issue raised at the town meetings was a need for "an abundant and unfailing water supply." Canton had outgrown its water supply and needed some improvements to meet present day requirements. A committee was formed to study the problems of flood control, water conservation, and additional dams.

Finally, citizens recognized the need for an "attractive business district." Immediately Canton launched a program of business stimulation and trade promotion. In March 1933, employment reached a low of 6,800 in Canton's factories. In January 1935, there were 15,000 on the industrial payroll. By May that number had increased to 17,800.

Chapter Seven

WORLD WAR II

"Yesterday, December 7, 1941, a date that will live in infamy, the United States of America was suddenly and deliberately attacked by the naval and air forces of the Empire of Japan."

~Franklin Delano Roosevelt

In a single day, the world changed forever. When Japan bombed Pearl Harbor, the United States was drawn into the largest war the world has ever known. As Americans listened to their radios in disbelief, President Franklin Delano Roosevelt addressed the nation. Across the country, a total of 16 million men and women mobilized to serve. Those left behind launched the largest and most comprehensive homefront campaign in history. Like many communities, the citizens of Canton were quick to pitch in for the war effort. Rationing became a way of life as supplies were redirected to the war effort. Canton's industries made significant contributions to defense production, creating a record to be proud of.

Before the United States entered the war, Canton's industries were already producing war materials for the Allies. In 1940, 68 local industries manufactured $140 million worth of products for the war effort. Timken was making bearings for the British and French before Pearl Harbor. It was this kind of increased production that pulled Stark County—and the nation—out of the grip of the Great Depression.

In December 1940, Timken announced plans for a $3 million expansion program at four plants, including Canton. The Army Ordnance Department needed gun barrels, and Timken engineers took on the project of developing a seamless tube gun barrel. The finished product could fire 7,000 rounds without a single sign of wear. The previous standard was a forged barrel that only lasted a few hundred rounds. In the early days of the war when national defense was a priority, Timken was also asked to produce anti-aircraft guns.

The same month Timken announced its expansion, Acting Secretary of the Navy James V. Forrestal selected Canton as the site for a $16 million bomb-proof naval ordnance plant that would employ 2,000. The Westinghouse Naval Ordnance Plant was built the following year on the corner of 13th Street and Raff Road SW. Navy officers who were stationed at the plant lived in the brick houses in the surrounding area, many of which were still standing over half a century later.

In January 1941, the Canton Board of Education approved a plan to extend vocational education in cooperation with local industries for the national defense program at the new Timken Vocational High School. In February plans for a $1 million defense housing program for Canton were announced. There would be 300 units for defense workers on 68 acres, adjoining Harter Heights (which later became the Don Mellet Housing Project). By March Canton's five major industries were devoting 65 percent of their output to national defense.

After Pearl Harbor, there was a rush to enlist in all branches of the armed forces. Canton's utilities and industrial sites went under wartime guard, and emergency plans were put into place to protect the city's vital systems. To safeguard the water supply, a round-the-clock watch was posted at water sources. Floodlights went up at the equalization basin at 30th Street and Cleveland Avenue, and the City Council voted to buy wire fencing at least 7 feet high around key water facilities. The federal government issued a proclamation banning all private aircraft and revoked all student pilot and instructor licenses.

Even as employment reached a peak of 33,340 and the gloominess of the Depression was fading into the past, Canton received news of the first local war casualty on December 12, 1941. Ensign Lawrence Williams had lost his life in the Pacific. By Christmas, 6,000 Americans had already been killed, including 2,300 at Pearl Harbor.

The most significant way a civilian could help contribute to the war effort was to pay close attention to consumption. The War Production Board and Office of Price Administration controlled all aspects of manufacturing, including defense production contracts, price regulation, and rationing. Federally mandated rationing of key consumer goods provided an adequate monthly amount per person to be used in the household, so that more products could be redirected to the war effort.

Fats were needed to make ammunition—one pound of fat contains enough glycerin to produce one pound of gun powder. And soldiers needed more food products like sugar and wheat to sustain themselves on the front lines. Nylon and silk were used to make parachutes, so stockings were hard to come by. Other products that were strictly rationed included sugar, coffee, red meat, canned goods, shoes, tires, and gas. Car production stopped completely in February 1942, and gas was made available to individuals according to their importance to the war effort. Drivers were given a rating—A, B, C, X, E, or T—to purchase gas. A national speed limit of 35 miles per hour was established to save gasoline. Sugar rationing began in March 1941, and sugar sales were banned the week before to prevent hoarding. Federal guidelines stipulated that each person would receive three pounds of sugar per month and no more.

Heating oil was also rationed, and people were encouraged to use wood stoves as an alternative. To help conserve coal, Canton held its first "brown out" in February 1945. Traffic Commissioner C.L. Deerwester said police noted about 50 brownout violations that were turned over to the Ohio Power Company for investigation. Violators who did not shut off illuminated signs and marquees were going to "have their power supply cut off if they persisted in ignoring the coal-saving measure."

Though they were not rationed, paper products, cigarettes, and coal were in short supply. The government had asked farmers to plant crops that were highly nutritious. As a result, watermelons were selling for a staggering $2.50 each! They were reportedly scarce and expensive during the summers throughout the war.

During the war, the Demonstration Committee of the Canton Women's Council of National Defense issued a cookbook called *War Service Recipes—Food Will Win the War*. The introduction stressed the impact a woman could have on the war by following the guidelines set forth by the government, and taking it a step further on her own:

> You would give your life for your country. You would scorn an American whose patriotism ended with waving flags, cheering the troops and standing up when the band plays. You want to serve your country. Are you willing to do what your Government asks? Are you willing to follow directions? It is the patriotic duty of every woman to follow the advice and recipes contained in this book. The price of 10 cents covers the actual cost of printing and paper.

The pages were filled with recipes for "meat extenders" and meatless entrees like baked eggs with cheese, cabbage rolls with rice, and Welsh rarebit. Women were urged to use less sugar in their tea or coffee and not to "let sugar remain in the bottom of your tea cup." Suggested sugar substitutes included molasses, honey, and syrups. Women were urged to "save sugar and fats all the time." The Girl Scouts were in charge of collecting kitchen fats.

The cookbook called on women to give up meat at least once a week, even going as far as to dictate that the meatless day should be Tuesday. "This means no meat of any kind on that day," the cookbook instructed. Research showed at the time that Americans were eating three times the amount of meat that they actually needed in their diets. Fish and poultry were recommended instead because they could not be shipped overseas.

The cookbook also encouraged the use of corn in cooking, because America was producing 30 bushels of corn per capita but was only eating one. "Corn is cheapest of all cereals with regard to nutritive values," the cookbook said. "The more corn we use the more wheat we have to send across the water." All of these sacrifices were framed within a heavy cloak of patriotism:

> The man ruled by appetite is not the free man. Perhaps the Kaiser thought we were ruled by appetite. If he did, no wonder he thought we were conquerable. We not only think, but know that we are unconquerable, that we will never acknowledge, nor submit to appetite or Kaiserism, or any other power save that of self-government, which is the gift of Almighty God, the Everlasting Father, the Prince of Peace.

As a means of self-imposed rationing, men wore "victory suits" that conserved fabric. There were no cuffs, slimmer trousers, and narrower lapels. Men also switched from the three piece suit to the two piece suit, shedding the extra material used to make the vest.

Conserving key wartime products was an excellent way to help on the homefront. But so was giving cold hard cash to help finance the war. Canton was chosen as a test site for a major defense stamp sale demonstration. In September 1941, one of the largest parades in the city's history took place with 3,000 marchers, 15 bands, and 100 trucks and floats. The demonstration won national attention from Washington, D.C. A $25 war bond could be purchased for $18.75. Defense stamps sold for 10¢ a piece, which could be saved until there were enough to buy a bond. *The Repository* newsboys began selling defense stamps.

While the nation was banding together on the homefront, changes in the military were just on the horizon. For the first time, women were allowed to enlist in the armed forces in special departments created just for them. There were now Army WACS (Women's Army Corps), Navy WAVES (Women Accepted for Volunteer Emergency Service), and Coast Guard SPARS (which was a name, not an acronym). There was no special name for women who joined the Marines. Recruiting campaigns aimed specifically at WAVES and SPARS began in Canton in March 1943. Those who enlisted were sent off to train individually. In July 1943, the army asked Canton to provide 1,800 women to enlist as dieticians, physical therapy aides, and aviation physiologists. They were given the rank of second lieutenant. By February 1944, there were enough local female enlistees that Canton formed its own WAVES unit—the Ida McKinley Platoon.

World War II

Rilla E. Thomas was one of those pioneering women who joined the war effort not by taking a factory job, but by joining the military. She enlisted in 1942 and was appointed junior clerk-stenographer with the Army Air Forces at Wright Field, Ohio. She recorded her thoughts about her experiences in a scrapbook. Her recollections of her days of service probably represent the thoughts and feelings of many of the women—and men—who were leaving home to join the war effort. Thomas wrote about the day she left with mixed emotions:

> I left Canton on the 10:45 train for Dayton. I was a little upset because Mama cried. Ethel went with me to the station and Elizabeth and Harold brought Tommy and Bobby down too. My first train ride. I wonder if everyone on the train knew that Ethel gave that reading of hers in pantomime and I laughed even when I felt like crying. I can see all those dear people now. Elizabeth was crying too. I hope I never forget how good she and Harold and Luella and Ralph, Mama and Ethel have been to me. When the train started I changed seats and then I sat opposite a woman and a man and two little girls. Those little girls were so sweet. At about eleven o'clock I ate some of the lunch Mama packed for me. She had fried a chicken and made sandwiches besides putting some pieces of cold chicken in it. The lunch also contained ginger bread another evidence of her love (she knows I am crazy about it). She also packed an apple which I ate for breakfast next morning.

When she got to Dayton, she immediately went to the YWCA to secure a room for the night. She was lucky enough to get one with a private bath. The next day she went out to Wright Field. "What a thrill that was. I thought because I had an appointment everything would be okay—what a laugh. After waiting to report for several hours I was told to report on the following Thursday."

Thomas needed a permanent room, so she went apartment hunting to kill the time before she started work. She found a nice place for $9 a week for room and board. After "playing around" for two days, she writes, "On Thursday I got up with every hope of getting started that day. But I didn't have my birth certificate. Was I disappointed. I had to go back to Canton, then on to Woodsfield, Ohio to prove my birth. It took almost every cent I had but I did get the necessary information."

Her career with the Army Air Forces lasted throughout the war. She was promoted several times during those four years. When she resigned on January 18, 1946, she was making $2,166, quite an increase from the $1,440 she started at in 1942.

Nadine Bluhm also served in the military during World War II. She was a WASP—Women's Airforce Service Pilot. Some women flew planes that towed targets that the trainees would shoot at. Others ferried planes across the country, so they could be shipped out or brought in for repairs. Though she was in uniform and was flying for the war effort, Congress refused to grant her and her colleagues military status. It was not until 1977—over three decades later—that the government officially recognized these women as veterans. Unfortunately, it was long after any of them could take advantage of the GI Bill. Bluhm was a founding member of the Military Aircraft Preservation Society (MAPS), located at the Akron-Canton Airport.

According to a booklet called *WACS in the Army*, "Every job which is not beyond the physical strength or endurance of women, and has suitable environment and working conditions, can be filled by members of the Women's Army Corps. The men of the Army are classified in 628 jobs. More than 400 of these jobs are suitable for women." The list included a variety of positions—some traditionally female and some traditionally male—such as mechanic, switchboard operator, radio operator, welder, riveter, cashier, bookkeeper, typist, stenographer, truck driver, baker, cook, dietician, and commissary steward.

The program for Graduation Exercises from the Army Administration Schools, WAAC (the extra "A" stood for Auxiliary, before the WACS were integrated into the Army) Branch No. 3, Class No. 3, May 19, 1943, listed three women from Canton—Mary A. Conner, Mary M. Uebing, and Mary J. Weis.

Before enlisting, Mary J. Weis had worked for attorneys Black, McCuskey, Souers, and Arbaugh. She also kept a scrapbook of her days in the service, which paints a vivid picture of life in the service. After induction, she was sent to Fort Oglethorpe, Georgia and became part of the 1st Company, 23rd Regiment. There were 80 girls on her floor, sleeping in double deck cots. She attended classes, marched, drilled, washed floors, cleaned latrines, took examinations, and did regular shifts of KP (kitchen duty).

Weis left Canton on March 4, 1943 on the Pennsylvania Railroad at noon. When she got off the train, she went by army truck for the last 9 miles of her trip. "A terrible raining night," she writes, "and my first night was one I shall never forget. Coal stoves in barracks. Toilet outside." At the end of the month, she received $29.65 as reimbursement for her fare from Canton, but she had only paid $13.12.

She and 300 other women left Fort Oglethorpe for the Arkansas State Teachers College on April 7. They arrived at 11:30 p.m. "Walked two miles to our new dormitory in rain. Called out at 6:00 a.m. Very tired girls." After a six week course, she graduated on May 19 and was assigned as a stenographer in Sheppard Field, Texas. Her background at the Canton law firm must have influenced her placement in the judge advocates office.

Weis was given a re-enlistment letter July 2. She wrote in her scrapbook, "not going to re-enlist." She received an honorable discharge and train fare home on August 13. She arrived home in Canton two days later at 10:00 p.m.

Relatively few women actually enlisted in the military. Most had a critical role to play on the homefront. As more men joined the military and left their factory jobs, it became apparent that there would be a shortage of men to fill in the gap. In September 1942, the U.S. Employment Office announced the need for more women workers to become trained paid employees in Canton's war plants. By 1944, Canton's major plants employed 15,082 women.

In March 1942, Price Control Administrator Leon Henderson froze rent citywide at the April 1, 1941 rate to help control inflation during wartime. All landlords who had increased rent during the preceding year had 60 days to comply with the new order.

Local civic organizations worked hard to contribute to the war effort, too. In March 1942 the American Legion scrap drive brought in 304,300 pounds, and the $2,627.82 in proceeds went toward the purchase of civilian defense equipment. Soon a city-wide program to pick up tin cans began. The Legion also launched a program to collect phonograph records to entertain the troops. Women met in the churches to roll bandages for the Red Cross, knit sweaters, and serve coffee in USO canteens.

The Canton YMCA extended free membership to any man in uniform, which included use of the showers, gym, and pool. Their 1942 Wartime Service Annual Report cited that 600 men had taken advantage of the offer since Pearl Harbor. They had given free cot service to 135, and provided overnight lodging in the dormitories at half the usual rate to 102 people. As of April 20, 1943, a total of 1,320 YMCA members had left to join the military. The YMCA also sent out "bulletins" that kept Canton's boys up to date on what was going on around Canton. The letters they received in return showed how much the soldiers cherished this connection to their hometown. They sent letters back to the YMCA like this one, written by Ed Bergman:

> Your Phalanx bulletin arrived here promptly on the 7th and was more than appreciated. I never realized when I was home how much this paper meant to the fellows away at Camp. Naturally I get clippings and news from my family and friends, but this bulletin gives you the added news that a fellow likes to hear. . . . Here at Croft there are a few weeks known as "Hell Week." I just went through one of them. I've been tired before, but this was a new experience. We spent the week at the rifle range. You are up at 4:30, hike 2 miles over hilly country to the range—you are there all day under a physical and mental strain—at dusk you return to camp for chow which is about

7:30 or 8:00. By the time your rifle is cleaned, it is lights out and you're ready for another day of the same."

The bulletins were mailed out a few times a year to all soldiers whose addresses were known. The YMCA also sent out Christmas cards.

Students were encouraged to contribute to the war effort as well. Canton schools even launched their own scrap iron drive. Schools that sold an outstanding number of war bonds and stamps were allowed to name a piece of military equipment, ranging from a bomber to a jeep—the more they raised, the bigger item they named. In 1943 Mt. Marie Academy was the first school in the city to win the Treasury Department's "Minute Man" flag by enrolling more than 90 percent of the students as War Bond and Stamp Buyers.

High school boys took over as substitutes for the U.S. Postal Service as more and more mailmen left their jobs to enlist. Kids were asked to walk to school whenever possible to free up bus space and help ease rush hour jams in bus service. Also, Canton City Lines introduced express lines that ran from Public Square directly to the war plants using a system of tractor type buses that could hold approximately 100 workers.

By the end of 1942, Canton's war plants were working around the clock, seven days a week. Diebold received Stark County's first Army-Navy "E" award in August 1942. The company devoted 98 percent of its activities to the war effort. They manufactured armored plate for aircraft and gun shields; shell containers and powder cases; hatches, doors, and frames for the merchant marines; anti-aircraft gun trailers; and armor plate bodies for over 36,000 scout cars. At the peak of the war, 2,900 were employed at Diebold's three Canton plants.

In 1943, city government instituted a 20 percent income tax, and the War Labor Board set fixed maximums for key war production positions:

Common laborers   70¢
Spot welders   80¢
Truck drivers   87¢
Radial drill press operators   92¢
Maintenance carpenters   95¢
Milling machine operators $1.00
Turret lathe operators $1.05
Millwrights, maintenance
electricians, and machinists $1.10
Tool and die makers $1.25

By the end of the year, more than 40,000 were engaged in wartime production in Canton's plants. And those employees were fighting the war with their wallets as well. Of the county's 89 firms who employed 100 or more people, 84 had a payroll deduction plan for war bonds in place in 1943. At least 17 companies were investing 10 percent of their payroll or more.

In 1944, Timken ran an ad that read, "Timken equipped bombers wipe out Nazi Bearing Production at Germany's three main plants, a mortal wound to German war pool." By that time, 5,268 Timken employees had been called to service. Fifty-one lost their lives. Women began to fill in the gap in the factory. Half the engineering force was female by the end of the war. At its peak, Timken was producing twice as much material as any other time in the company's history. They were building deck guns for submarines, railroad cars to move coast guard guns, and propeller blade ball bearings for aircraft. To meet the escalating demand, Timken went from three shifts of 40 hours each to four shifts. Employment rose from 8,000 before the war to 18,000.

Timken added a plant in downtown Canton, across the street from Timken Vocational High School. High school boys and girls from the school worked five hours a day behind glass walls making bearings. The public was invited to come and see the amazing partnership between the company and the high school. Timken also hired 18 blind people to help with the worker shortage, because many office workers had taken part time jobs in the war plants. Although many high school graduates planned to join the military, those who did not were bombarded with offers from Canton's industries for jobs in the war plants.

Hoover won accolades for its war efforts as well. In 1944, two of its ads were included on the list of the 100 most outstanding wartime ads published that year. One of them was their Christmas ad. They used slogans like "Let's Fight With Our Homes to Shorten the War," "Give Her a War Bond and You Give Her the Best," and "The Neighborly Spirit of Sharing." Hoover dedicated 10 acres of company property for the employees' free use as Victory Gardens, earning them awards from The National Victory Garden Institute in 1943 and 1945. The company also introduced a Car Club to encourage employees to car pool with one another to save gas. They hosted blood donation campaigns, scrap drives, and loaned employees to government agencies whenever they were needed.

Hoover employees produced a staggering amount of war materials—including over 26 million point-detonating fuses and 17 million other war items. The last vacuum cleaner rolled off the lines on April 30, 1942, and the factory was completely retooled to make tanks, planes, ships, gunmounts, and artillery pieces. Hoover also produced M48 and M51 fuses, incendiary bomb parts, shot bags, plastic helmet liners, life boat inflator mechanisms, parachutes, propeller motors, and air blower units.

One of the most significant contributions was the 35 million components needed to build the VT radio fuse, the second most top secret weapon of the war, next to the atomic bomb. The VT radio feature made it possible for the fuse to explode its projectile when it was approximately 70 feet from its target, eliminating the difficulty of actual hits or timing for distance to a fraction of a second. The VT radio fuse helped combat the German buzz bomb and the Japanese suicide bombers.

The production of the VT radio fuse was so top secret, only ten Hoover employees knew the end products into which the component parts were assembled. It wasn't until after the war that any information at all was released to the public about this important project.

Like Diebold, Hoover won the Army-Navy "E" Award five times, which earned them the right to fly the Army-Navy "E" Flag with four stars on it.

At the beginning of the war, the government limited the number of vacuum cleaner orders Hoover could process. By April 1942, the government forced Hoover to stop vacuum cleaner production altogether. It would be three years before the next vacuum cleaner would be built. Available parts had to be distributed carefully. The stockpile ran out just as the war was ending. Hoover was prepared for a quick transition back to peacetime production

Union Metal Manufacturing Company became the first Canton war industry to win the coveted maritime commission "M" for superior production in July 1943. They were already flying the Army-Navy "E" flag and the Minute Man flag for employee purchases of war bonds. This scenario was played out in factories across the city. Everyone was working hard to ensure that the United States would emerge victorious.

War production reached a staggering $375 million at the end of 1944. Paper was in short supply for military and government use, so *The Repository* stopped running advertisements in the Wednesday edition. Stark County's fourth War Loan Drive in 1944 ended 45 percent over quota. Civil defense activities continued throughout the war. In 1943 *The Repository* reported a successful daytime air raid drill, the first Canton had held. The streets were deserted.

To create a distraction from the double shifts and self-sacrifice, people turned to the movies as an escape. Such classics as *Casablanca*, *The Maltese Falcon*, *The Grapes of Wrath*, *Arsenic and Old Lace*, and *Double Indemnity* came out during the war years. Besides going to the movies and attending USO functions, most people just stayed home. Parlor games and card playing enjoyed a spectacular renaissance during the war period.

Everyone agreed that positive news from home would help bolster the resolve of the young men in the military. To do their part, *The Repository* ran a regular column called "A Letter from Home: The Week's News for Men Serving Our Country's Flag" throughout the war. Each column began "Dear Harry," and was designed to be cut out and mailed to the servicemen by their families. Topics ranged from reports on war work at home to updates on various high school sporting events. Each week was crammed full of interesting tidbits for the boys in uniform.

In March 1943, the column talked about the excitement over the Victory Gardens, saying there would be more amateur gardeners in Canton than ever before:

> People really woke up to the situation when they began to study their ration books and found they can buy about one can of vegetables a week providing they don't want to use their coupons for canned fruit juice, raisins, catsup or any of the other many rationed foods. They discovered that if they are going to have beans and tomatoes and such things on the table frequently they better grow them for themselves.

Though the ground was still frozen, the reporter described the people of Canton reading seed catalogs and drawing plans for their spring plantings. Nationwide Americans cultivated 20.5 million Victory Gardens, producing one-third of all the vegetables consumed that year.

Though writing letters to servicemen was strongly encouraged, in June 1943 the column cautioned friends and families not to try to communicate with homemade code. "Information passed in this manner might do great harm, the Navy says. It also says that codes are easily detected and that their use to avoid the censors is punishable by severe penalties."

News of Japan's surrender reached Canton on August 14, 1945. A grand celebration followed. By August 16, telegrams to stop war production arrived in Canton, rendering millions of dollars worth of contracts null and void. Thousands of workers were laid off. The city held a victory parade on September 3. Of the 31,810 Stark County residents who served in World War II, 670 never made it home.

Chapter Eight

SUBURBANIZATION

"The separation between urban and rural has practically disappeared. What used to be two modes of life, city and country, have merged into one—the suburban."

~Stark County Historian E.T. Heald

When the war was over, like the rest of the nation, Canton's businesses needed to transition themselves into a peacetime economy. Timken began making plans as soon as war was over on the European front. By the end of the war, they were ready to supply the new production of cars and trucks. The Model 27 Hoover debuted on September 4, 1945.

Despite the cancellation of war contracts, the boom in wartime production had boosted Canton's community all around. In a 1940s promotional booklet designed to entice industries to relocate or open branches in Canton, the writers boasted that within a 25 mile radius, a variety of raw materials could be found in Canton—clay, coal, sandstone, limestone, sand and gravel, and salt. Fabricated materials like alloy steel, bearings, castings, iron, electric motors, forgings, dies and tools, rubber products, paper products, and diesel engines could also be found within 25 miles of the city. The booklet also outlined the civic advantages of Canton, including 35 grade schools (8 parochial), 5 high schools (1 parochial), 2 large hospitals with a total of over 500 beds, 2 private maternity hospitals, 1 tuberculosis sanitarium, and churches of several denominations—75 Protestant, 7 Catholic, and 2 Jewish.

Built in 1938 and given as a gift to the Board of Education by H.H. Timken, Timken Vocational High School was touted as "the finest and best equipped vocation school in the country." The school offered day trade classes in drafting, printing, welding, pattern making, electricity, machine shop, sheet metal, auto mechanics, secretarial courses, restaurant training, retailing, dress making, accounting, cosmetology, and commercial art. The school would also work with employers by offering special classes to meet their needs. During World War II, over 5,000 workers were trained in 25 different occupations at Timken. They also sponsored a Trade Extension series for part-time students in bricklaying, plumbing, and carpentry. McKinley, Lincoln, and Lehman High Schools offered the usual variety of college prep courses designed for kids who planned to earn their degrees.

Suburbanization

As previously noted, in 1860 only 21 percent of Stark County's citizens lived in the three largest towns of Canton, Massillon, and Alliance. But by 1920 that number grew to 71 percent. Since then, the rise of the automobile—and well-maintained roads to drive them on—swung the trend back the other way. By the 1950s, the suburban population was larger as a whole than the population of any one city in Stark County.

This mass exodus from the city has been studied by some of the greatest historians of our time. The reasons are complicated and simple. Since the founding of this nation, the ultimate dream of every American was homeownership. Canton was founded on the principle of westward expansion, where settlers had the opportunity to buy their own land. As an agrarian society shifted to an industrial one, so did the ideal residential dream. People weren't aspiring to be farmers anymore. In 1920, 90.8 percent of Stark County's land was devoted to farming. By 1945, that number had decreased to 72 percent. People wanted to be successful businessmen or industrialists. And where was the best place to make that dream come true? The city, of course. With limited transportation available to them, the only alternative was to live close to the business section of town. As the urban population grew, the rural areas were being swallowed up. Stark County was no longer the #1 agricultural county in Ohio.

Enter the automobile. Once an efficient roadway system became a national priority, the size of the world seemed bigger—and smaller—all at once. Now people could travel greater distances at their own leisure, without relying on public transportation. They were free to go wherever, whenever they wanted. People started to reexamine city life, and they found it crowded, polluted, congested, and generally distasteful. And the paradigm shifted again.

The ideal American dream became homeownership in the newly booming suburban sprawl. It was far enough from the city to provide a peaceful respite from the cares of the work-a-day world, yet close enough for a reasonable morning commute.

In Canton, the affluent suburban developments of Hills & Dales and Avondale were the first to provide the ideal suburban location for the city's wealthiest citizens. Gone were the days of expansive houses with rolling lawns on Market Street. Gradually the center of town became devoted to business—offices, shopping, restaurants and the like. And one by one, the gorgeous mansions of Canton's early residents were razed to make room for more parking garages and office buildings.

In the 1950s and 1960s, the automobile revolutionized the shopping habits of consumers—not only in Canton but nationwide. For the first time, people began straying away from the downtown shopping district to suburban shopping centers. The postwar economic boom meant people had more money to spend, and after two decades of deprivation, they were ready for some serious shopping.

CANTON

According to Stark County Historian E.T. Heald, the American housewife of the 1950s would "rather drive a mile than walk a block." The snarling traffic downtown and struggle for a parking place was not nearly as appealing as the prospect of driving a few miles to a shopping center with an expansive parking lot and a variety of stores in one place.

The first three shopping centers in Canton were Country Fair, 30th Street Plaza, and Mahoning Road Plaza. The first stage of County Fair began in October 1950 and was open for business in July 1951 with 12 stores. Kroger, Woolworth, and Gray's Drug Store were anchors. There was also a branch of Harter Bank & Trust Company. The second stage was opened in September 1953 with ten more stores, including Halle's and Thurin. Stephen Baytos of Youngstown bought 16 acres for the future 30th Street Plaza in 1950. The shopping center opened in October 1952 with 17 stores and 2,500 parking places. Construction on the Mahoning Road Plaza began in August 1954 on the site of the old McKinley Airport. It was finished in March 1955.

Several other smaller shopping centers were popping up in Canton during this time as well, including John's Shopping Center on Cleveland Avenue NW, Fulton Road Shopping Center, Tip Top Mart at the corner of 30th Street and Martindale, and the Lake Cable Shopping Center.

In the mid-1960s, Stern & Mann remained an anchor in the downtown shopping district. They were one of only 300 stores in the country that were still locally owned and operated and had become an icon in the community. Everyone in Canton recognized their logo on boxes and bags and probably had something hanging in their closets with a Stern & Mann label.

The store celebrated its 75th anniversary in 1962 with splashy full page ads in *The Repository*, highlighting the history of their company. "From the very beginning," the ad read, "the first little store grew and prospered. The growth of the city . . . has also been rapid, providing exceptional opportunities for imaginative, progressive retailing service . . . and leading the way for the distinctive fashion specialty store which Stern & Mann's was destined to become." The ad continued, "The Third Generation, forming the branches of this great family-owned and operated store, draws energy and inspiration from their grandfathers and fathers."

Their special 75th Anniversary Sale featured "merchandise as fresh as daisies" and "as welcome as a burst of sunshine." The ad also mentioned that there was "ample parking space" in any of the downtown "Park and Shop" lots, indicating marketing competition with the new suburban shopping areas with vast parking lots.

Though the company was enjoying success, the winds of change were blowing just over the horizon. The changes Stern & Mann would make during this time were indicative of the dawning of a new era, one that would forever change the composition of cities and towns across the map, including Canton.

In 1964, Stern & Mann opened its first branch at the 30th Street Plaza, marking the landmark store's first move toward leaving downtown. When announcing the plans, Vice President Robert M. Mann said, "We are cognizant of the fact we are locating an additional outlet away from the downtown center but we are facing another kind of living today. With easy access and parking, combined with growing suburbs, the concept of retailing has been shifting to suburban shopping centers." Even with the new expansion plans, Mann stressed that his business would maintain a presence in downtown Canton and would not change a thing in the original store.

In 1968, Stern & Mann opened another branch called the "Little Shop" inside the Harvard Clothing Store at Mellett Mall (now Canton Centre), featuring a scaled back line of women's fashion merchandise. That soon closed because of its small size. In 1970, another branch at Belden Village Mall opened. In 1974 the company ventured out of Canton for the first time by opening a branch in Alliance on West State Street.

In 1969, Stern & Mann completed a major renovation to its downtown department store, spending $500,000 to modernize. They eliminated four large display windows to add a larger misses' sportswear shop, men's department, and show salon. The new décor was dubbed "modernistic art" and reflected the multicolored pop culture of the 1960s. They rearranged existing departments to maximize their space.

The automobile not only revolutionized people's shopping habits, it also transformed the social scene, which revolved around drive-in restaurants and movie theaters. The first carhop was Avalon's, located at the time quite a distance out of town on Cleveland Avenue. Brothers A.A. "Skyes" and Gerald Thoma built it in 1935 and named it after a Pacific Island paradise they had heard about on a visit to the West Coast.

The menu featured frozen custard (a novelty at the time), sandwiches, and their signature burger "Big Sis." Cruising was elevated to an art form in the 1950s, and kids would "Buzz the A" to see what was going on, even if they didn't have any money or weren't particularly hungry. There were two other branches of Avalon's at Ninth Street and North Market Avenue and at Dueber Avenue and West Tuscarawas Street. The original Avalon closed in the 1970s to make room for a Wendy's. Other drive-in restaurants that have faded into fond memories are Lujan's, Eckard's, and Waterloo.

There were lots of other things for kids to do in the 1950s. Kids 12 and under could fish in the city parks' streams and ponds, which were restocked with fish every year. In the winter, ice skaters enjoyed themselves on the frozen pools of water. There were organizations for all kinds of interests—archery, bowling, bridge, Civil

Defense, dancing, "ham" or amateur radio, flowers, golf, history, poetry, and a host of other hobbies.

Throughout the first half of the twentieth century, there was a shift from men's secret societies to more service luncheon clubs for businessmen. Once a week these groups would meet for fellowship and to encourage high standards for business and professionalism. Their main purpose was to assist in humanitarian efforts and raise money for benefit projects. The Rotary was started in 1914, Kiwanis in 1918, and the Lion's Club in 1920. These clubs were wildly popular in the postwar years.

The 1950s were also a time of dreaming about the future. "Out with the old and in with new" was the phrase of the moment. Preservation efforts were scattered and terribly old-fashioned for the dawn of the Space Age. During this era, some of Canton's greatest landmarks were razed in the name of progress. The old, stately City Hall had become outdated and was much too small for the growing city's government. It was torn down in April 1959 to make way for a "startlingly modern City Hall with glass and stainless steel curtain walls," according to Stark County Historian E.T. Heald. The Canton Memorial Auditorium was built in the 1950s on the corner of 11th Street and Market Avenue. The old City Auditorium had been declared a fire hazard and was not used after 1938.

Even time was progressing in the 1950s. On November 8, 1950 Cantonians voted 24,382 to 19,575 to support year-round Eastern Standard Time. Clevelanders voted to observe Daylight Savings Time again the next year. A *Repository* article stated "Two years ago when Canton Council was slow in enacting legislation for fast time, Canton became an island in a sea of fast time until the change was made."

After World War II, Canton was the largest city in the country without a college. With a deluge of GIs returning from the war poised to take advantage of the GI Bill, the city needed a college. From 1946 to 1950, Kent State operated a quasi-branch campus using classroom space at McKinley High School, the YMCA for health and physical education classes, and the former Timken home at 1014 North Market Avenue for a Union Building. There were 2,704 students, 61.2 percent of which were not GIs, taught by 119 full- and part-time instructors. In 1950, the voters of Canton shocked the college by voting down the Timken Foundation's offer to give the city the $500,000 Timken Estate as a gift for a college home. From 1950 to 1952, there was no Kent extension in Stark County. In 1953, Kent started offering evening classes that were broadened in 1957 to include all of the basic required courses. In the fall of 1958, 4,234 students enrolled.

Malone College opened in 1957 on 54 acres of land formerly occupied by the Canton Infirmary. There were 250 students that first year. Originally founded in 1892 as the Cleveland Bible College by J. Walter and Emma Malone, the college was forced to relocate when its land was needed to construct a new expressway. Canton was selected as a new site. On February 14, 1956, the college changed its name to Malone in honor of its founders. Ground was broken on November 4, 1956.

Walsh College also came to Canton from another location when LeMennais College moved here from Alfred, Maine in 1959. In March 1958, Brother Patrick and Brother David of the Brothers of Christian Instruction closed on a $100,000 purchase of 50 acres on East Maple Street near Market Avenue. The cornerstone was laid in December 1959. The college was originally renamed Canton College, but the name was changed in honor of Reverend Bishop Emmet M. Walsh of the Youngstown Diocese. The college opened in 1960 with 68 students. By 1963 enrollment had increased to over 300.

Canton celebrated its sesquicentennial in August 1955. The community extravaganza lasted for a whole week, with theme days that included Festival of Faith Day; Homecoming and Governor's Day; Fraternal, Nationality, and Civic Clubs Day; Youth Day; Industry Day; Labor and Agriculture Day; and City and County Day.

A beauty contest crowned 14 Sesquicentennial Princesses and two Queens—Nancy Riegel, Miss Canton Sesquicentennial, and Ann Hadjian, Miss Stark County Sesquicentennial. A fashion show demonstrated costumes from the pioneer days in various categories classified as "authentic" and "non-authentic."

The men were not left out—they held their own beard growing contest. Local barbers served as judges in several categories, such as longest full beard; blackest, whitest, and reddest beards; most comical beard; best mutton chops; best goatee; and neatest handlebar mustache. There was also a booby prize for the man who tried the hardest and accomplished the least. The winners got something they were sure to appreciate—a jar of shaving cream!

A highlight of the festivities was a nightly pageant at Fawcett Stadium called Canton-O-Rama. The performances featured 19 "episodes" on topics like "This is the Canton Story," "Of Books, Slates, and the Hickory Stick," and "An Era of Progress: The Iron Horse Comes to Canton." Hundreds of Cantonians participated in the cast of the show. By the end of the night, visitors learned the entire history of Canton, from Native Americans to World War II.

There was a Moonlight Cotillion at Meyers Lake one night from 9:00 p.m to 1:00 a.m., sponsored by the Junior League. Ball attendees swayed to the music of Danny Thompson's Orchestra for $3 a couple. All of the downtown stores featured antique window displays. There was a baton twirling contest, drum and bugle corps competition, historical tours of the city, and fireworks every night. Berger

Manufacturing (a division of Republic Steel), Timken, Hoover, and Ford Motor Company offered tours of their facilities. Ohio Power had demonstrations of electric and gas cooking.

The sesquicentennial celebration concluded on August 20 with the largest parade in the history of the city. Jets screamed across the sky and the air raid sirens went off to start the parade. Military units, band music, floats, horses, and cars belonging to members of the Antique Automobile Club and the Horseless Carriage Club filed down city streets. Some of the floats were quite elaborate, costing thousands of dollars to build. Timken sponsored a three unit red, white, and blue float with a large replica of a roller bearing. The Hoover float featured women sweeping with various models of vacuum cleaners. The Greek community float highlighted classic Greek architecture with men and women in flowing robes. The Canton Board of Education's float depicted a scene of students at the first Union School juxtaposed with a modern classroom setting. Other spectacles included an 8-foot chicken, street cleaning equipment from 1885, and early post office vehicles. Despite 90 degree temperatures, a crowd of 100,000 came out in honor of Canton's 150th birthday.

Chapter Nine

THE MODERN ERA

In the latter half of the twentieth century, there was a national trend toward a service oriented economy. Industrial jobs gave way to banking, retailing, insurance, medicine, law, and government. Manufacturing jobs have been consistently moving overseas, where the overhead is far cheaper for the companies, expanding their profit margin significantly. This trend has resulted in increased unemployment for skilled factory workers and an increased focus on education to better prepare young men and women for the professional careers available to them in a modern economy. Gone are the days when Junior followed his father into the steel mill. There are few steel mills left.

In the late 1950s, Canton was still trying to shake its mafia underworld image from the events that had occurred decades before. When word spread that the National Football League (NFL) was looking to build a new Pro Football Hall of Fame, Canton's leaders jumped at the chance to bring it to town. Canton was a contender since the first professional league had been organized here. But Latrobe, Pennsylvania was a strong possibility too, since that was where the first person was paid for playing football. There were also other large cities thrown into the mix—Green Bay, Detroit, and Los Angeles all wanted the Hall of Fame too.

The Repository played a key role in garnering community support. In December 1959, they ran a story with the headline "Pro Football Needs a Hall of Fame and Logical Site is Here." Sports writer Chuck Such wrote:

> It was here in Canton that professional football was born. Here, the first
> pro football league was organized on September 17, 1920. . . . Canton has
> a right to expand its chest and pop a few vest buttons. It was the cradle of
> pro football. However, the project will require a combined Herculean effort
> on the part of civic and sports leaders, business and industry, and perhaps
> more important, just plain fans.

Henry Timken saw the story and committed whatever resources necessary to organize a campaign for Canton. Canton also had a friend in Paul Brown, the head coach of the Cleveland Browns and former Massillon coach, who had substantial influence in the NFL.

The NFL was looking for someplace that had historical significance to the game, financial backing, and easy access from a major highway. History Canton had; it was money and land that they needed.

Business rallied around the idea. Though Timken was not much of a football fan, he loved Canton and wanted to do something positive to renew the city's tarnished reputation as a haven for gangsters, gambling, and prostitution. He pledged $250,000, but that was not enough. The NFL was not in a position to contribute, since the organization was fighting for survival itself. So a 12 member steering committee met and began raising money in the community. They held their first meeting in February 1960. They had one year to create a package that would impress the NFL and bring the Hall of Fame to Canton.

Most of the businesses in Canton contributed to the fundraising efforts, with big bucks coming from both Timken and Hoover. In total, they raised $378,026. The city owned some land just off the highway and agreed to lease it to the Hall of Fame for $1 a year for 99 years. With land secured, the package was complete.

On January 25, 1961 they pitched their case to the NFL. After three long months of waiting, the news finally came. The Pro Football Hall of Fame was coming to Canton. "Canton was in the majority by a considerable margin," an NFL spokesman said after the selection. "There was no opposition to Canton."

Work began at once to make the Hall of Fame a reality. It was decided that a circular building would maximize space on the original 14 acres. The dome that has become a local landmark was not a deliberate design element of the building. To create head room for visitors walking up a ramp to the second floor, a dome was added that just happened to look like a football. The ground-breaking was held in 1962.

With the building near completion, they still had no artifacts to put in it. An intensive search for relics of the game began. The Hall of Fame acquired memorabilia from the Canton Bulldogs, Jim Thorpe's blanket and 1912 Olympic blazer, a ledger from the Allegheny Athletic Association showing the first payment to a football player, Knute Rockne's Massillon Tigers pro team helmet, the oldest known football dating to 1890, and the NFL's "birth certificate"—the minutes of that first meeting of the American Professional Football Association in a Canton car dealership on September 17, 1920. So when they opened on September 7, 1963, there were some things to show visitors.

The Hall of Fame founders pitched the idea of a Hall of Fame Game, modeled after the one held annually at the Baseball Hall of Fame in Cooperstown, New York. The

NFL loved the idea. They decided teams from outside Ohio should play in the first game, so the New York Giants and St. Louis Cardinals were invited to Canton. They played to a 21–21 tie. There were so few fans at that first game, photographers were asked to take pictures from strategic locations to make it look like there was a big crowd.

The enshrinement gallery was designed for 34 individual tributes, to be chosen by the sports media. They based the annual induction size of two or three players on the Baseball Hall of Fame. It would have been adequate for at least two decades, if the "charter class" had not consisted of 17 players. So they were running out of room from the very beginning. The first expansion took place just a few years after it opened.

By 1971, the NFL was gaining popularity and was in a financial position to fund the third building. As more people became interested in football, attendance increased at the Hall of Fame. In 1973, 330,029 people came through the doors, a record that still stands. The sky was the limit! That is, until the oil embargo crushed tourism nationwide. In October 1973, the Organization of Petroleum Exporting Countries (OPEC) announced plans to limit production of oil, which caused prices to skyrocket. The subsequent energy crunch kept most Americans close to home for the duration of the crisis.

The 1980s saw a rise in visitation once again, as oil prices returned to normal and tourism came into its own as an industry. In 1985, the Hall of Fame inducted what has become known as the best class in Hall of Fame history. Inductees included: Joe Namath, quarterback for the New York Jets; OJ Simpson, running back for the Buffalo Bills; Pete Rozelle, NFL commissioner; Frank Gatski, lineman for the Cleveland Browns; and Roger Staubach, quarterback for the Dallas Cowboys.

On August 19, 1991, the 5 millionth visitor walked through the turnstyle. Robert Dean, a gangly 14-year-old from Portland, Oregon who was touring the Midwest with his family, was showered with a $1,000 shopping spree in the museum's shop, a lifetime membership, and his very own trading card with his picture on it. The family didn't even have plans to visit the Hall of Fame that day. According to family legend, Robert's father Steve missed the exit on the turnpike and decided to take the scenic route. They ended up on Route 62 and decided to stop at the Hall of Fame.

More than $10 million was invested in the Hall of Fame in its fourth decade. The facility has expanded to 83,000 square feet, including the state-of-the-art Game Day Stadium Theater which shows a film on the previous season's Super Bowl champions on a 20 by 42 foot Cinemascope screen. The head coach of the featured team is invited to come to the debut.

In 2003 a new $1.7 million enshrinement gallery opened. The busts were reorganized by class, and a series of six interactive touch screens were added that show highlight clips from each Hall of Famer's career. The enshrinement is now televised live on ESPN, and each new inductee seizes the moment with a speech. In 2002, the enshrinement ceremonies were moved from the front steps of the Hall of Fame to Fawcett Stadium to accommodate the huge crowd who came to see Buffalo Bills star Jim Kelly receive his yellow Hall of Fame blazer.

Community volunteers and Hall of Fame officials work together to organize the annual Hall of Fame Festival, drawing thousands of visitors from across the country.

An event that required the same kind of coordination was the nation's bicentennial. In 1976 our country's 200th birthday sparked all kinds of celebrations across the country, with over 23,000 projects and 27,000 events planned nationwide. Canton hosted several bicentennial celebrations all over town.

Canton's Bicentennial Weekend, over the Fourth of July, began with a public viewing of a very special statue at the Cultural Center. Mayor Joseph Rey of Colmar, France flew across the ocean just to present Mrs. W.R. Timken with a 101-year-old, 47-inch clay model of the Statue of Liberty. It was made by Auguste Bartholdi, the sculptor who created the real Statue of Liberty. He made about five different "practice" models before erecting the big one in 1886. In 1976, only three of them survived, and the one given to Canton was in the best condition. It was not an exact replica of the Statue of Liberty. Bartholdi changed the folds of her gown on the real statue, and the numerals on her tablet are not the same.

How did such a treasure find its way to Canton? The Timken Company had a branch factory in Colmar, France that employed 1,300 people. Over the years, the Timken International Fund had donated large sums of money to the French town for educational and cultural purposes. To show their gratitude—and celebrate America's bicentennial—the mayor of Colmar presented Mrs. Timken with this priceless statue. Pierre Burger, curator of the Bartholdi Museum in Colmar, also came to Canton. He said the statue had been on display in Colmar since 1922, and before that it was in Bartholdi's apartment in Paris.

Mrs. Timken was the president of the Cultural Center's Board of Trustees at the time. In the same ceremony, she donated the statue to the Cultural Center and it went on display at the Canton Art Institute (now the Canton Museum of Art).

Other bicentennial events included a Bicentennial Tour of Homes, an International and Ethnic Bicentennial Festival at the Memorial Auditorium sponsored by the Canton Bicentennial Commission, displays at the Canton Bicentennial Headquarters downtown, an old-fashioned picnic sponsored by the Women's Auxiliary of the Stark County Historical Society (now the McKinley Museum), and "Colonial Fair Days," featuring pioneer arts, crafts, songs, stories, and games. There was a display of historic newspaper front pages at the Mellett Mall on topics like the assassinations of Lincoln,

Kennedy, and McKinley; General Robert E. Lee's surrender ending the Civil War; the Great Chicago Fire; the sinking of the *Maine, Lusitania,* and *Titanic;* the *Hindenburg* wreck; and Nixon's resignation. Special projects included a major restoration project for the McKinley National Memorial.

The Canton Art Institute, Stark County Historical Society, and Junior League of Canton collaborated to create an exhibit called "The Bicentennial Exhibit, 1776–1976: 200 Years of the United States of America and Canton, Ohio." The exhibit was done in two phases: the beginnings to 1850, and 1850 to 1976. It included a look at America's history, focusing on topics specific to Canton's artifacts, art, and architecture.

The "largest flag in all the world" (a 53 by 120 foot flag made by the women of Canton to help sell Liberty Bonds) that had been such a source of pride during World War I turned up missing and could not be used for the bicentennial festivities. The Canton Telephone Pioneers of America, comprised of 500 employees who had worked at Ohio Bell for at least 20 years, agreed to underwrite the cost of a new flag at a cost of over $2,000.

Canton's main event was Festival 76, which featured booths and demonstrations throughout Stadium and Monument Parks. Guest speakers included Congressman Ralph Regula, Stark County Historical Society President Gervis Brady, and Canton Mayor Stanley Cmich. Visitors could see "Flower Display of Designs" at the Canton Garden Center, a pioneer living demonstration by the Boy Scouts, and a tennis tournament. Admission to the Stark County Historical Society was half price—50¢ for adults and 25¢ for children.

The commercial nature of most of the festivities sparked some dissenters to re-christen the national celebration the "Buycentennial." Indeed, the souvenirs available for the centennial in 1876 were of much higher quality than the plastic Uncle Sam banks and Liberty Bell pencil sharpeners available for the bicentennial. But by the 1970s, our society had been completely transformed into a haven of consumerism.

While people may be willing to spend more disposable income on cheap souvenirs, most consumers want to save time and stress when it comes to travel. Local airports are more likely to offer convenient parking options and fewer hassles than metropolitan airports. In 1987, the Akron-Canton Regional Airport was the fastest growing airport in the country with 700,000 passengers flying in and out annually. Millions of dollars had been poured into expansions and reconstruction. Canton was lucky to have such a facility nearby. In fact, they almost blew it completely when talk of an airport first surfaced before World War II.

In the 1930s, Hitler had begun his systematic takeover of Europe. Before the United States entered World War II, Germany had already invaded Poland, Austria,

CANTON

Czechoslovakia, Denmark, Norway, Holland, Belgium, France, and England. Fearing worldwide domination, President Franklin Roosevelt ordered the Civil Aeronautics Administration (CAA) to get America ready for air defense. The CAA was a division of the Department of Commerce and was given the responsibility of enforcing safety in aircraft construction, licensing pilots, regulating passenger rates, and assisting in airport construction through an act of Congress in 1938. In September 1940, the CAA allocated $500 million for a long range plan to develop airfields across the country. Ohio was to receive $15 million for 104 airfields.

The CAA chose Canton to receive $231,600 for surveying and site work for a Class 2 airfield, a designation that meant it could handle planes with a capacity of 20 passengers. The military needed an airfield in Stark County to act as a distribution center for new fighters and bombers, so the CAA approved $2 million for the construction of an airport near Canton. All the city had to do was provide the land. The military required three runways, each 5,600 feet long and 150 feet wide, on at least 800 acres.

Debate dragged on about where to buy the land. Finally in December 1942, the city council voted to use $200,000 from the Timken War Profit Tax revenues to purchase land for the airport. The money was originally supposed to help pay for a sewage plant and repairs for the Auditorium.

But it was too late. The CAA was tired of waiting for Canton to make a decision, so it selected land in Summit County instead. The Canton Chamber of Commerce was dumbfounded. They tried to salvage the loss by proposing a bi-county effort between Stark and Summit Counties, only to discover that joint county ventures were illegal in Ohio. Legislation was introduced in March 1943 to change this law, but the measure failed. Luckily a Stark County businessman found an obscure law allowing joint county enterprises, so the state legislation was bypassed.

Again, the CAA and the army were fed up with the delays in Stark County and President Roosevelt nixed the whole project. After bombarding Washington, D.C. with phone calls of protest, the project was again approved. The groundbreaking took place on October 6, 1944, just over the county line in Summit. In February 1946, four airlines announced plans to leave the Akron Municipal Airport for Akron-Canton Airport, which had larger planes and longer runways. Dedication ceremonies were held in October 1946. American, Eastern, and United landed large airplanes on the brand new runways. Private planes were also housed at the new airport.

The airport experienced its first plane crash on December 28, 1948 at 7:58 p.m. Eastern Flight 758 lost its landing gear as it touched down and skidded down the runway. There were no injuries. The first fatalities happened almost a year later on

November 4, 1949 when a twin engine DC-3 crashed in a wooded area near the airport, killing three men.

The airport celebrated its fifth anniversary with an air show on October 13, 1951 sponsored in part by the Junior Chamber of Commerce for a crowd of 150,000. The Civil Air Patrol piloted the planes. That show was free of tragedy, but on Memorial Day 1955, stunt pilot Paul Anderson lost his life at the age of 29 when his plane failed to come out of dive and crashed in front of a crowd of 2,500.

In 1962, the airport made further improvements with new radar and runway lights and increased staff. They advertised new features including concrete parking lots, restful lounges, modernized check-in and baggage areas, quality dining services, moving sidewalks, and an observation deck.

Despite these enhancements, passengers seemed to prefer Cleveland Hopkins to the Akron-Canton Airport. Before the renovations in 1959, 89 percent of the travelers in Stark and Summit Counties were going to Cleveland. Afterwards, the number dropped to just 70.7 percent. Cleveland had more flights and was easier to get to, especially for residents on the northwest side of Akron. What the Akron-Canton Airport needed was a highway.

Construction on Interstate 77 began in 1957. Funding for the project was split 90 percent from the federal government, 5 percent from the state, and 5 percent from the cities it ran through. By 1966, I-77 was completed, and the airport launched a marketing blitz to entice passengers to the facility. They mailed 200,000 brochures, gave out 100,000 free placemats to restaurants, and distributed windshield stickers with the message "Use Akron Canton—your nearest jet airport."

The airport continued to struggle in the 1980s with the recession and an air traffic controller strike. Deregulation of commercial aviation encouraged major airlines to move operations to high traffic points. The future looked bleak.

Then 29-year-old Fred Krum took over as airport director in 1981. He started to turn things around. Under his leadership, the airport embarked on a $15 million expansion project, receiving a $2.1 million grant to extend the runway in 1982. The number of airlines flying out of Akron-Canton started to increase.

Today Akron-Canton continues to compete with Cleveland, but it is managing to hold onto its slice of the market, even as the airline industry struggles to recover from September 11. The airport continues to be run by four trustees from each county who serve on the Akron-Canton Regional Airport Authority Board.

The airport was not the only facility to undergo sweeping changes in the last quarter of the twentieth century. The shift away from the downtown shopping district continued throughout the postwar period and peaked in the 1960s and 1970s with the opening of Canton's two indoor malls—Canton Centre (formerly Mellett Mall) and Belden Village.

The Mellett Mall began as a dream for a group of homeowners. The Mellett Housing Project, named after slain newspaper man Don Mellett, was a series of barracks-like apartment buildings constructed by the federal government in the 1940s as homes for workers at the Westinghouse Naval Ordnance Plant. (Years later the plant was razed to make room for commercial development between Raff Road and Whipple Avenue on the south side of Tuscarawas Street.) The owners of these homes joined together to develop a shopping center. They were ordinary people—industrial workers, truck drivers, salesmen, and clerks—who pooled their money and took a chance.

In 1963, Mellett Homes announced plans for a 300,000 square foot mall on 33 acres on the southwest corner of West Tuscarawas Street and Whipple Avenue SW. Their goal was 48 units. Early on they received word from J.C. Penney that it would be an anchor store for the project. The M. O'Neil Company of Akron (now Kaufman's) made a commitment to the mall in April 1965. With two major stores, plans for the mall were well underway. Originally the mall consisted of six separate buildings in an open-air configuration. A roof was added later.

A four-day opening celebration for the $7 million project was held in August 1965. Wilbur Cooper, promotion manager for the Mellett Mall Merchants Association, was master of ceremonies. Television personalities Skitch Henderson, a regular on *The Tonight Show*, and Dody Goodman made appearances at the festivities.

By its first anniversary, Mellett Mall was home to Gray Drugs, Betty's Beauty Salon, Cleveland Fabric Shops, Norman's Shoes, Sherwin-Williams, Troy Laundry and Dry Cleaning, Woolworth's, London's Candies & Ice Cream, and many other stores. That summer Montgomery Ward opened a 3,100 square foot store at the mall, with departments furnishing appliances, televisions and radios, tires, batteries, and a large assortment of specialty merchandise in addition to the 130,000 items offered in their catalog. The store planned to expand in 1967. In a *Repository* article in July 1966, W.W. Shine, the company's Cuyahoga Falls district manager, said "Montgomery Ward has been attracted to Canton by the strong customer acceptance we have throughout the area, combined with the community's present and future economy."

In the next few years, several downtown department stores—including Harvard Clothing Store and Rapport's Inc.—opened "satellite" stores in the Mellett Mall. Though many reaffirmed their commitment to downtown, it was becoming clear that the future of the retail industry was concentrated in the growing suburbs.

The Modern Era

Mellett Mall celebrated its anniversary in 1968 with quite a bit of fanfare. A highlight was Flapper, a 330-pound whale "of high intelligence," who performed every 30 minutes in a 25,000 gallon tank. The mall also displayed the captured Zis limousine that was once owned by Cold War villains Joseph Stalin and Mao Tse-Tung. Only 15 had been built and were reserved for high ranking Russian officials. Stalin had reportedly given the car to Mao in 1951 when he was in Moscow for talks on China's role in the Korean War. Mao gave it to his army for use as a staff car where it was subsequently captured by the U.S. Army. It was a composite of a 1939 Packard and Cadillac and was the only one known "outside the Iron Curtain."

The stockholders of Mellett Homes Inc. voted to sell the mall to an anonymous Cleveland family in 1981. Forest City Management Company was contracted to operate the mall. In 1988, the company completed a major $16 million renovation and held a contest to come up with a new name to go along with their new image. Over 6,000 entries were received and judged by two company officials. Canton Centre was chosen because it clearly identified the location of the mall and implied that it was the retail "center" of town.

Some members of the community were outraged. They believed the Mellett Mall should remain as a lasting memorial to Don Mellett. To help ease the transition, Forest City set up a $2,000 scholarship in Mellett's name to be awarded annually to a Stark County resident who was pursuing a career in journalism. Money would be raised through the coin fountain inside the mall, and the rest would be contributed by Forest City. *The Repository* advocated the idea, saying "naming a mall after him was a nice gesture, but a scholarship is a better one." Sadly, the scholarship only lasted a few years before a dismal financial picture forced the company to discontinue the fund.

The 1988 renovations included a new food court, ceiling, flooring, lighting, trees, and benches. They improved drainage and reconfigured the parking lots and interior roadways to facilitate traffic flow.

In 1997, several new stores came to the mall, including Bath & Body Works, Kodak Image Center Solutions, Amerimortgage, and Staples. Camelot Music, Radio Shack, Nickelodeon, Bountiful Harvest, and American Dental Center remodeled and expanded. Despite these improvements, Canton Centre continued to compete with Belden Village, which was booming as a result of expansion in Jackson Township.

Plans for Belden Village were announced on June 23, 1966, with Higbee's and Sears as its anchor stores. Founders Henry Belden and Herbert Strawbridge had gone to school together as kids. Strawbridge went on to become the vice chairman of the board of the Higbee Company, and Belden was in the oil and gravel business.

CANTON

Years later, they met for a meeting and Belden noticed a map on Strawbridge's desk with circles around towns in northeast Ohio. "Looks like you're planning to build a store in Canton," he said. Strawbridge said that a store in Canton was at least a decade away. Then Belden told him that he, his brother Marshall Belden, and their sister Elizabeth Martin owned some land in Jackson Township and would be interested in a joint venture.

The two men agreed that Belden would buy up property around the land he already owned, while Strawbridge worked on convincing the Higbee Board to build a store in Canton earlier than planned. They went to local businessmen to pitch their idea. Henry Timken was absolutely against it. He believed that a new mall should be built downtown, not out in Jackson. Strawbridge argued that downtown should remain the business and financial center and that the time was right to build new retail outlets in other parts of town. At the same time, Sears pulled out of their downtown lease and was looking for a place near Canton to build a new store. The pieces all fell into place, and the mall opened on October 1, 1970.

The chain stores in both malls began to transform the retail industry in Canton. In the 1990s, an era came to an end as one of the last locally owned department stores closed its doors for good. In 1985, the Stern family sold their interest in the company to the Manns, ending four generations of joint ownership of Stern & Mann. That was the first of many changes for the store.

From 1988 to 1991, the store experienced drastic restructuring. A sharp decline in downtown shopping in the 1960s and 1970s led to increased emphasis on satellite stores. When Tri-State Realty Company, which owned its building, informed Stern & Mann they wanted to convert their downtown building into office space and would not be renewing the store's lease, it was time for a change.

In 1989, their lease on the Alliance store was up and they chose not to renew it. They opted to try the Akron market instead. Their lease at Belden Village expired around the same time, and mall management wanted to divide up their space and use some of it to attract new stores. This would have left a space that was too small for Stern & Mann, so they withdrew from that location as well. "You can't become a shop when you've been a store," Robert Mann said.

Although three stores closed during this period, two new ones opened at Thursday's Plaza and Fairlawn Center. The new locations offered the same quality merchandise Stern & Mann's had become known for. Despite a recession and widespread consumer uncertainty during those years, the store relied on its heritage and name recognition to stay afloat. Many department stores had already given way to smaller specialty shops that filled the malls. The Stern family decided to close the stores in the early 1990s.

As more and more locally-owned stores were replaced by national chains, the character of Canton began to change. In 2002, Belden Village became a branch of the conglomerate Westfield Shoppingtown. Sarah Ferguson ("Fergie"), former British Royal, came to Canton to promote the "new" mall. Large stores like Wal-Mart, Sam's Club, Home Depot, Target, Dick's Sporting Goods, David's Bridal, and Kohl's began to spring up in the rapidly growing area of Jackson Township.

Downtown Canton had become inconvenient for shoppers and businessmen alike. In a 1991 *Repository* article, Tom Funk, president of T.K. Harris Commercial Sales, said the Belden Village had "easy access to I-77, plenty of free parking, restaurants and stores. Downtown has high parking rates, congested one-way streets, and a lack of aesthetics." The cost of new building projects downtown became an expensive proposition as real estate prices climbed, with the added demolition expense of removing an existing building. Few businesses were willing to take on a restoration project in a historic downtown building when they could just buy land out in Jackson and build what they wanted.

In recent years, there has been some effort to revitalize downtown Canton. Beautification projects and joint tourism efforts have helped to raise the profile of the downtown area. Several restaurants and small stores still operate, serving the business community that still calls downtown home.

In the mid-1990s, development began to creep north on Dressler Road with the construction of several large shopping centers, including The Strip at the intersection of Dressler Road and Portage Street. The Strip capitalizes on the new concept of a "mega" strip mall—a traditional shopping plaza on a much larger scale. The Strip houses commercial giants like Lowe's; Bed, Bath & Beyond; and Borders, as well as a variety of free-standing restaurants like Joe's Crab Shack, Longhorn Steakhouse, and Chuck E. Cheese. Giant Eagle was one of the first stores to open on The Strip with a grand opening on November 12, 1996. The 91,000 square foot store is twice the size of the former store at 5555 Dressler Road. The new store features expanded bakery and prepared food departments, as well as a sushi bar, gourmet cheese counter, and an elegant wine section. "Extras" include a dry cleaner, one hour photo shop, a bank, and a cell phone company. Iggle Entertainment is a full service video store, offering all the latest releases in movies and video games.

By the year 2000, real estate was booming in Jackson as well. New construction was on the rise as the migration further from the center of the city continued. One extreme example is the community of Glenmoor, with multimillion dollar homes situated on a Jack Nicklaus signature golf course. Nicklaus was paid $1 million to design the 18-hole course. The centerpiece of the gated community is the clubhouse, located in the former Brunnerdale Seminary. Empty lots sold for $60,000 to $90,000. Golf course memberships were sold for a one-time fee of $30,000 each, with annual dues of $3,450. Some of Canton's top executives and government officials call Glenmoor home.

Canton of today could not be more different than the clearing in the woods Bezaleel Wells bought in 1805. As the world changes, so does Canton—for better and for worse. Many of the changes Canton has seen over the past 200 years have mirrored national trends. As the national economy makes a painful transition from an industry-base to service-oriented jobs and professions, communities like Canton have suffered.

But Canton's past reads like a litany of who's who in business and industry. This city has been the home of many prominent citizens, from President William McKinley and industrial leader H.H. Timken to aeronautic pioneer Frank Lahm. Canton has had a history of attracting important people and businesses to town with the promise of opportunity and advancement. Though factories and amusement parks have closed their doors, the incredible expansion of Jackson Township and the continued growth of tourism are a sign of things to come for this city.

Images of Canton's past may have vanished from the landscape, but their memory lives on in the pages of history. As time continues to march into the future, new personalities will emerge to lead this community to new heights. People have come and gone over the past 200 years, but they have all left their mark on the history of this city. Bezaleel Wells would be proud of everything Canton has achieved and all that is yet to be accomplished.

BIBLIOGRAPHY

"10-block square signaled beginning of Canton." *The Repository*. 4 July 1976, 50.

Albacete, M.J. *Architecture in Canton, 1805–1976*. Canton: The Canton Art Institute, 1975.

Balint, Ed. "A man without a home." *The Repository*. 8 June 2003, sec. B1.

Brown, Jeffery D. and Raymond D. Fete. *Meyers Lake Revisited*. Canton: Daring Books, 1985.

Brown, Gary. "Moment In Time: Avalon as it was under the sun." *The Repository*. 15 April 2001.

Burwell, Robert L. *They Walked on Wings: A History of Early Stark County Aviation*. Canton: Saracen Publications, 1988.

Galloway, Barbara and David Knox. "Where's the saturation point?" *The Akron Beacon Journal*. 8 October 1995.

Gibbs, James W. *From Springfield to Moscow: The Complete Dueber-Hampden Story*. Philadelphia, PA: James W. Gibbs, 1986.

"Glenmoor is green oasis of golf in Jackson." *The Independent*. 28 March 1992.

Heald, Edward T. *Brief History of Stark County, Ohio*. Canton: Stark County Historical Society, 1963.

———. *The Stark County Story, Volume I: The Cities, Towns and Villages of Stark County, Ohio*. Canton: Stark County Historical Society, 1949.

———. *The Stark County Story, Volume II: The McKinley Era*. Canton: Stark County Historical Society, 1950.

———. *The Stark County Story, Volume III: Industry Comes of Age*. Canton: Stark County Historical Society, 1952.

———. *The Stark County Story, Volume IV, Part I: Free People at Work*. Canton: Stark County Historical Society, 1955.

———. *The Stark County Story, Volume IV, Part II: The Suburban Era*. Canton: Stark County Historical Society, 1958.

McElroy, Richard L. *William McKinley and Our America*. Canton: Stark County Historical Society, 1996.

McKinley High School Senior English Students. *What You Know Could Fill a Book*. Canton: McKinley High School, *c.* 1985.

Porter, Todd. "Linked from the Start: NFL and Canton have grown up together." *The Repository*. 3 May 2003, sec. C1.

———. "Hallowed History: Pro Football Hall of Fame 40th Anniversary Special, 1994–2003." *The Repository*. 25 May 2003, sec. CC1.

———. "Hallowed History: Pro Football Hall of Fame 40th Anniversary Special, 1984–1993." *The Repository*. 18 May 2003, sec. CC1.

———. "Hallowed History: Pro Football Hall of Fame 40th Anniversary Special, 1974–1983." *The Repository*. 11 May 2003, sec. CC1.

———. "Hallowed History: Pro Football Hall of Fame 40th Anniversary Special, 1964–1973." *The Repository*. 4 May 2003, sec. CC1.

Spencer, Ralph K. "Avalon Closing Ends Era." *The Repository*. 14 November 1972.

Stark County Regional Planning Commission. *An Inventory of Historical Sites and Structures*. Stark County: Stark County Regional Planning Commission, 1976.

William McKinley Post No. 25. *Honor Roll and History*. Canton: William McKinley Post No. 25, 1932.

Young Men's Christian Association. *Wartime Service Annual Report 1942*. Canton: Young Men's Christian Association, 1942.

INDEX